ATROPOS PRESS
new york • dresden

General Editor:
Wolfgang Schirmacher

Editorial Board:
Pierre Alferi
Giorgio Agamben
Hubertus von Amelunxen
Alain Badiou
Judith Balso
Judith Butler
Diane Davis
Chris Fynsk
Martin Hielscher
Geert Lovink
Larry Rickels
Avital Ronell
Michael Schmidt
Victor Vitanza
Siegfried Zielinski
Slavoj Žižek

© 2019 by Wanyoung Kim, PhD
Think Media EGS Series is supported by the European Graduate School

ATROPOS PRESS
New York • Dresden
151 First Avenue # 14, New York, N.Y. 10003

all rights reserved

Cosmophenomenology: The Alterity and Harmony of Consciousness as Quantum Energy

Wanyoung Kim, PhD

TABLE OF CONTENTS

Acknowledgments	8
Abstract	9

Chapter 1. Introduction: Materialism and Its Implications

I.	The In/Finite Universe	13
II.	Non-Anthropocentrism	24
III.	Panenpsychism	34

Chapter 2. Cosmophenomenology

I.	Lifeworld and Givenness	37
II.	The Constant of Consciousness	43
III.	Quantum Entanglement	53
IV.	Topology of Selfhood	61

Chapter 3. Quantum World and Harmony

I.	(An/)Harmonics	77
II.	Leibniz's Monadology and Quantum Physics	82
III.	On Affirmation	93
IV.	The Archetypal Psyche	97

Chapter 4. The Multiverse

I.	With and Against Goethe	102
II.	Deleuzian Multiplicity	105
III.	Embracing Quantum Paradox	106

Chapter 5. The Physicists' Heaven

I.	Dimensions	108
II.	Brahman and Collective Consciousness	112
III.	Types of Matter	113
IV.	Spacetime	114

Chapter 6. The Void as Necessary for Creation

I.	Black Holes and Dark Matter	117
II.	The Meaning of Singularity	120
III.	Multiplicity and the Psyche	123

Chapter 7. Collective Consciousness Throughout History

I.	Hegel and Eastern Thought	129
II.	Transcendentalism	131
III.	Walter Benjamin and *Jetztzeit*	133

Chapter 8. *Atman* and Neuroplasticity

I.	Symbolic Order and Psyche	135
II.	Flexibility and Adaptation	139
III.	Destructive Plasticity	146

Chapter 9. Death and Afterlife: The Beyond as Liminal

I.	Bardo Theol (Tibetan Book of the Dead)	149
II.	Monads and Pure Consciousness	151

Chapter 10. A Cosmophenomenology of Heaven

I.	The Givenness of Near-Death Experiences	159
II.	A Para-Phenomenology of Perception	162
III.	Refuting the Skeptics	167

Chapter 11. Conclusions   170

Bibliography   186

Acknowledgments

I worked on this book's manuscript in the coastal Eastern seaboard of Incheon, South Korea, and back home in Ann Arbor, Michigan. I frequented dusty shelves in my grandfather's library while breathing in the air of the Eastern seaboard, listening to the call of seagulls and pigeons. I also wrote indoors in the silence as it snowed. This manuscript has been made possible by my family's support. I thank my professors, Wolfgang Schirmacher, Chris Fynsk, Catherine Malabou, and Philippe Beck. I give thanks to all persons whose work I cited, especially Stuart Hameroff and Roger Penrose, Max Tegmark, and those whose testimony I have quoted from the Near Death Experience Research Foundation.

Abstract

My book is primarily about metaphysics: the ontology of consciousness. I theorize that consciousness, otherwise known as the soul, is the emergent property of quantum energy, not ordinary matter, that retains its form as quantum information regardless of the death or decay of ordinary matter. Quantum energy is polymorphous, expressible as biophotons of ordinary light as well as waves. The wave of quantum information is the form consciousness takes up as quantum energy or Brahman, while biophotons are atman, the form consciousness takes on in neurons.

The constitution of consciousness as quantum dark energy is radical because it also explains why waves change to photons in the presence of consciousness. Dark energy is surmised by physicists to be Einstein's cosmological constant because it shapes the relativity of spacetime, dictating the behavior of atoms and light photons and also existing in a void. The mistake of materialists is to equate the 4% of the universe that dark energy literally moves about, to the force itself which constitutes over 70% of the universe[1]. Dark energy and ordinary matter are highly different in constitution, but

---
[1] My position regarding consciousness is emergentism involving dark energy.

curiously interact psycho-kinetically. Dark energy is responsible for the very expansion of space between galaxies[2].

In place of classical physics which cannot be used to study quantum energy, I use the approach of cosmophenomenology to study the ontology of consciousness. Cosmophenomenology, a term first coined by Danish theologian and philosopher K.E. Løgstrup, is used to describe an approach that extends the traditional phenomenology of Edmund Husserl to include the relation between human beings and reality as a whole (nature) from the point of view of the universe, rather than simply human-to-human relations. As such, it extends beyond anthropocentric and speciesist views of consciousness.

I am using the approach of cosmophenomenology specifically to discuss the alterity and harmony of consciousness as a quantum level of dark energy, and the necessary relation it has with quantum mechanics and multiple worlds, topics which either phenomenology or cosmological physics alone are inadequate to account for. I will discuss Husserl's alterity and Leibniz and Goethe's harmony.

---

[2] "Have Dark Forces Been Messing With the Cosmos?" in *The New York Times,* February 29, 2019: "String theory suggests that space could be laced with exotic energy fields associated with lightweight particles or forces yet undiscovered. Those fields, collectively called quintessence, could act in opposition to gravity, and could change over time — popping up, decaying or altering their effect, switching from repulsive to attractive."

My book centers around the primordial form of consciousness as quantum dark energy which has a continuation of existence after a person's bodily or physical death. After existence in *atman* as dark energy in microtubules, the property of consciousness reorders itself as quantum information that retains the prototypical properties to revive memory when it is reconstituted back into microtubules via incarnation. The First Thermodynamic Law states that energy neither goes out of being nor comes into being. Consciousness is not dependent on the existence of matter, space, or time, although it interacts with these variables. As a fundamental force, dark energy would retain its form regardless of space or time. The phenomenology of consciousness after death is a vegetative and holographic state, although consciousness, as mentioned, is fully reconstituted.

I compare the continuation of quantum information properties of consciousness, although not consciousness itself after death in the Orch-OR (Orchestrated Objective Reduction) theory of Sir Roger Penrose and Stuart Hameroff with that of the monadology in Leibniz. Both theories concern the inscribing of consciousness as quantum information in small structures which allows this information to pass on into different realms of the universe after death. The Quantum Immortality theory also discusses the passing on of consciousness into a different universe which allows it to evade death. In an infinitely expanding universe not confined by space or time, there would potentially be an infinity of such multiple universes and their dimensions. I have preceded the discussion of these theories with a thorough explanation of quantum mechanics and the interaction between the dark energy of consciousness and matter in the universe. Dark energy is the very motivating force of material phenomena.

Without dark energy, matter would be motionless. I follow the discussion of consciousness with a discussion of the metaphysical states of harmony and disharmony in the quantum world and cosmology of Goethe and Leibniz. After mentioning Leibniz, I compare Blanchot's neuter and his position on the impossibility of death to the alterity of consciousness in a Brahmanic and quantum entangled state. I also supplement my view of post-death consciousness in testimonies of near-death experiences and as a view of the intermediate state in Tibetan Buddhism.

Chapter One. Introduction: Materialism and its Implications

I. Materialism and the In/Finite Universe

The majority of this book is what constitutes the majority of the universe, dark energy (68-73%[3]), considered by physicists to be the cosmological constant. Materialism is the theory or belief that nothing exists except matter and its movements and modification[4]. A faulty or tautological definition uses the root of a word to define itself. It further begs the question

---

[3] Due to the impossibility of computing the size of a constantly expanding universe, which is further discussed, we can only refer to its constituents by mass. Hence, we can say that the majority of the universe is dark energy, and only 4% of it ordinary matter.

[4] The other part of materialism is the view of physicalism where "mental phenomena are caused by material or physical forces" (ibid.), which I will discuss in further chapters.
 If everything is energy or its instantiation as matter, we can consider the entire universe, including consciousness, is some manifestation of energy patterns in the void. We must then consider the positions of panpsychism and its refutations with vitalism and emergentism. I have countered panpsychism, the view where everything is alive because it is aenergic, with the view of panenpsychism, addressed later in this chapter, where only certain things contain energy. While panpsychism is a simpler system, panenpsychism better accounts for the distinction between alive and inert things. Vitalism is also necessary for my position because not all things containing energy are alive; a rock is not considered alive in the sense that a person is. We can also consider emergentism, where due to the composition of energy, we cannot say that a conscious organism's system is merely the sum of its parts. I will further discuss emergentism in Chapter 3, with the view of Jaegwon Kim.

of what we mean by "matter". Ordinary matter comprises only 4% of the universe, while dark matter is 27% and dark energy 69%.

I will differentiate ordinary matter from energy, its primordial form or supposed modification, as well as dark matter. The historical definition of matter is something that can be studied by the methods of empirical science and is regarded as something tangible. Dark energy in addition to dark matter is known in the absence of ordinary matter, and is known by its interaction with matter. The ordinary materialist, in talking about matter, is claiming a metaphysical stance about something that only constitutes a small fraction of the entire universe.

Materialism would require that the universe be fully measurable because it is only composed of ordinary matter. We know dark matter and dark energy by their functions as gravitational glue and space expansion, respectively. The latter function of dark energy is especially important to my book.

Dark matter and dark energy only have their names to serve as categorizations filling gaps in materialism, or even classic physicalism's capacity to explain phenomena. Materialism is problematic because it is incorrect to say that energy and the dark form of matter, are a modification of matter. Rather, $E=MC^2$ states that matter is a modification of energy, as energy condensed. It is furthermore impossible to derive dark matter from matter, as dark matter is only known in the very absence of matter itself. It is thus *altered* to matter, or its opposite. Much of what constitutes the universe is *altered* to matter in the sense it is matter's absence. For these numerous reasons I find materialism problematic and incoherent.

It is likely that the universe is an unfathomably[5] large entity, rather than one that is infinite in size. The universe is continuously expanding at variable rates[6]. There are a number of ways to calculate the size of the universe,

---

[5] By "unfathomably" I mean that not all parts of the universe are observable from afar or open to space exploration due to the sheer distance or obstacles such as black holes. This means that science must make conjectures or hypotheses, and that science cannot discern absolute truth.

[6] Hawking and Penrose, *The Nature of Space and Time*, p. 89: "Why is the universe so close to the dividing line between collapsing again and expanding indefinitely? In order to be as close as we are now, the rate of expansion early on had to be chosen fantastically accurately. If the rate of expansion one second after the big bang had been less by one part in 10^{10}, the universe would have collapsed after a few million years. If it had been greater by one part in 10^{10}, the universe would have been essentially empty after a few million years. In neither case would it have lasted long enough for life to develop."

Dr. Riess in "Have Dark Forces Been Messing With the Cosmos" in *The New York Times,* February 29, 2019: "This is not the first time the universe has been expanding too fast."

although physicists have not agreed upon any one method. The size of the universe is dependent on a number of factors, most especially its rate of expansion (Hubble constant) as well as the crucial factor of the observability of light as quantum waves. It would make sense that 68-73% of the universe comprises dark energy, for expansion is an important feature of the universe: what would otherwise be seen as the space between atoms because it is the very creating force of space. The primary role of dark energy as a moving force of ordinary matter will be brought up with respect to consciousness.

In 2013, the European Space Agency's Planck space mission, by measuring and studying the background of microwaves[7] from the earliest version of the universe at the time of the Big Bang in terms of baryonic[8] acoustic oscillations, pieced together a highly accurate, detailed, and up-to-date map of the universe's oldest light when the universe was just 380,000 years old. This

---

[7] Hawking and Penrose, *The Nature of Space and Time*, p. 95: "The quantum excitations of the gravitational wave modes will produce angular fluctuations in the microwave background whose amplitude is the expansion rate (in Planck units) at the time the wave function froze."

[8] "Baryonic" refers to ordinary observed matter such as protons or neutrons. Note that this only applies to 4% of the universe that is observable, and not to dark matter or energy which is known in interaction with ordinary matter. Once again, science cannot discern total truth and must rely on conjecture.

light has expanded along with the universe. The map which converts sound to visual format shows that the universe is 13.8 billion years old.

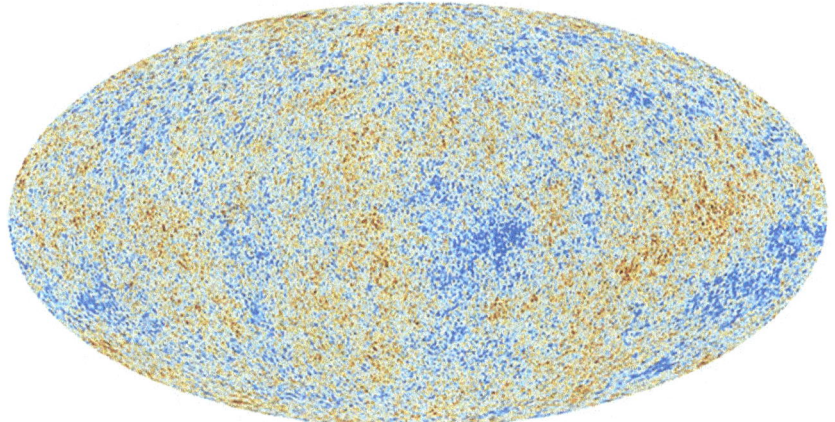

Figure 1: Planck's Cosmic microwave background

The observable universe[9] is 13.8 billion light-years in radius or 27.6

---

[9] Anthony Ashton in *Harmonograph,* p. 6 mentions "Robert Fludd's 17th century engraving of a monochord [which] shows the notes of a scale arranged in exponential fashion along a single string, with each assigned to planets or elements. There is a hint here of what we can think of as the 'great monochord' of the universe, also on a scale, this time stretching from a single quantum fluctuation at the bottom, to the observable universe at the top, passing through the various 'octaves' of atom, molecule, quantities of solid, liquid, and gaseous matter, creatures great and small, planets, star and galaxies." There is harmony as well as disharmony, with dissonance tied to complexity.

billion light-years in diameter, meaning that astronomers' telescopes can see 13.8 billion light-years outwards in each direction into the depths of the universe or locate a galaxy 13.8 billion light-years away. If there were no expansion of the universe, this would put the observable universe at 27.4 billion light-years in diameter, although scientists are aware that the universe is much larger due to constant expansion[10].

The universe has been expanding ever since its point of coming into being in the Big Bang,[11] and will continue to do so indefinitely and perhaps infinitely

---

[10] Pascal states in *Pensees*, Fragment 230: " The whole visible world is only an imperceptible speck in nature's ample bosom, no idea comes near it. We have puffed up our conceptions beyond imaginable space, we have only given birth to atoms compared with the reality of things. It is an infinite sphere whose center is everywhere, whose circumference nowhere." He is correct in a number of assumptions. As we have mentioned, he is right about the small size of the observable universe, and in stating that the universe is infinite in size because it is infinitely expanding. In accordance with the calculation of radius and diameter, he is also right it is a sphere whose parts are expanding in proportion with its former dimensions.

[11] Louis Auguste-Blanqui states in *Eternity by the Stars*, "The Universe is a Sphere, whose center is everywhere and its surface is nowhere." Expansion indicates that the universe has no true center or no fixed circumference. It also means that there is ultimately no fixed point in outer space that you can occupy throughout time. If we assess the Universe in terms of its expansion throughout time, it is true that the diameter or surface of the universe is a series of concentric circles with newly

due to dark energy. Galaxies are constantly drifting apart from one another. Although we could say that it is impossible to calculate or measure the space between galaxies due to constant expansion, we can also state that space is not a constant variable[12], according to Einstein's theory of relativity, where space and time are both constructs whose measure are not absolute[13]. This would imply that we live in a universe not absolutely constrained by the mere tools of

---

forming center-points and increasing diameter. A lack of surface means we cannot assess the universe in terms of topological layers.

[12] Hegel, *Encyclopedia Philosophy of Nature, §254*, "Time is characterized as a negative unity." In other words, time has no inherent measure. Max Tegmark, *Our Mathematical Universe*, p. 147: "Einstein allows space to stretch and produce more volume from nothing, without taking it from someplace else. In practice, this infinite universe might look something like a subatomic black hole from the outside." We can say that there is entropy in the universe due to the fact that space is not a constant, and this would disprove the notions of the universe being harmonic.

[13] Robert Lanza, *Biocentrism*, p. 115: "Space is not a constant, not absolute, and therefore not inherently substantive. By this, we mean that extremely high speed travel makes intervening space essentially shrink to nothingness." Hawking and Penrose, *The Nature of Space and Time*, p. 103, also state: "The positive curvature of spacetime produced singularities at which classical general relativity broke down." Hawking and Penrose believe that gravity allows space and time to proceed linearly, with a beginning and end. They have refuted general relativity in the opposite way as Henri Bergson, who believes that time is inherently relative.

measurement of the physical world by which we come up with[14] numbers such as the age of the universe[15]. If spacetime is one construct, and dark energy is responsible for space creation between galaxies by telling atoms to repel one another, this would also beg the question of whether dark energy as the fundamental constant of the universe is also responsible for the relativity or inconsistency of time, an issue I will address in Section II of Chapter II. There is much more dark energy than matter, and there is no limit to the number of times atoms will repel under dark energy's influence, meaning that the potential infinity of space allows for infinite dimensions and worlds.

---

[14] Alfred North Whitehead, *Process and Reality,* p. 209: "Human intellect 'spatializes the universe'; that is to say, that it tends to ignore the fluency, and to analyse the world in terms of static categories." This is a refutation of Immanuel Kant, who believes that spacetime is an intuition of the mind.

[15] Carl Sagan, *Cosmos, p. 10:* "The size and age of the Cosmos are beyond ordinary human understanding." We can relate this to the concept of universal truth or Brahman, which is transcendent: Subhash Kak, "Concepts of Space, Time, and Consciousness in Ancient India", p. 2: "Within the Indian tradition it is believed that reality, as a kind of a universal state function, transcends the separate categories of space, time, matter, and observation. In this function, called Brahman in the literature, there are all categories including knowledge."

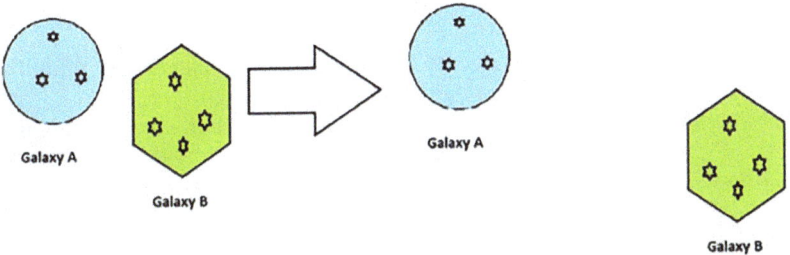

Figure 2: The Universe's expansion throughout time

A constant rate of expansion means that no matter what galaxy you happen to be in, there are other galaxies always drifting away from yours[16],[17]. A constant rate of expansion since the time of the Big Bang would indicate that a spot that was once 13.8 billion light-years away is now 46 billion light-years apart. That would put the diameter of the universe, including its unobservable

---

[16] The movement of galaxies can be likened to bread with raisins baking, or a balloon being blown up.

[17] Max Tegmark, *Our Mathematical Universe*, p. 141, on eternal inflation: "Inflation generally refuses to stop, forever producing more space." This relates to the existence of multiverses. In Chapters Nine and Ten I discuss how the infinite space of multiverses allows room for the quantum information that consciousness is preserved as, and supplements the Quantum Immortality Theory.

portions, at 92 billion light-years. Astronomers using NASA's Hubble telescope have discovered that the universe is expanding 5-9% more quickly than normal which would cause the true size of the universe to be bigger than 92 billion light-years in diameter. They believe that this greater than normal rate might be a now-inherent feature of the universe rather than a glitch. One possible explanation for this is that dark energy — the mysterious force known to be accelerating the cosmos — is driving galaxies farther apart with greater intensity. In this case, the acceleration of the universe may not have a constant value but rather be variable over time. As we conceive of a universe with an indeterminate size and perpetually changing centerpoint[18], we can turn back to the map derived from the cosmic microwave background.

It has been clear that the role of sound and the quantum waves of early light have been crucial in determining the size of the universe. "Any measurement made in cosmology can be formulated in terms of the wave

---

[18] If the centerpoint of the universe constantly changes, this means that unlike the view of Blanqui or Pascale, we cannot know if the universe is a sphere or whether it is some other shape that is irregular. Once again, science is unable to discern absolute facts about the universe.

function"[19],[20]. This means that these measurements can be harmonic or anharmonic, the latter meaning whatever is not abiding by simple harmonic motion. However, even in anharmonic situations, we can approximate them to harmonic ones using the wave function, a fact that is also analogically true for events in the universe. This means that overall, harmony is said to occur despite anharmonic activity. If the measurements can be done in terms of harmonics, we could say that the universe corresponds to a type of mathematical harmony, as in Goethe's *Faust*. This harmony will be further discussed in Chapter III.

---

[19] Hawking and Penrose, *The Nature of Space and Time*, p. 86

[20] Hawking and Penrose, *The Nature of Space and Time*, p. 92: "To see what the no-boundary proposal predicts for the homogeneity and isotropy of the universe, one has to consider three-metrics which are perturbations of the round three-sphere metric. One can expand these in terms of spherical harmonics. There are three kinds: scalar harmonics, vector harmonics, and tensor harmonics." We approximate the universe to be in the shape of a sphere, even if we are unsure of its actual shape or location of its centerpoint.

II. Non-Anthropocentrism

Humankind has traditionally been thought of as the center of the universe, whether in terms of a fixed centerpoint on earth, or in terms of the certainty of human measurement or perception[21]. (It includes anthropomorphism, the tendency to attribute human characteristics to objects.) Anthropocentrism is an approach that however outdated scientists and philosophers seek to avoid in their thinking, because it is part of an innate tendency of the mind, not just an approach found in history. However, the flaw of anthropocentrism is that things are not as they appear to the human senses or perception. It may be inevitable to phenomenology itself. Anaximander

---

[21] Protagoras in Plato's Theaetetus,152a stated: "Man is the measure of all things". This may indicate that there is some anthropomorphism or anthropocentrism that is inevitable, even in cosmophenomenology, and lead us to question if we can ever escape anthropocentrism as much as we consider it a duty to overcome and go beyond it.

formulated a view of a geocentric universe[22] with circular orbits[23] that is also found in the Ptolemaic system and was used by the Church until its acceptance of the Copernican system championed by Galileo. However, the difference between Anaximander's universe and the one conceptualized by physics is that Anaximander's is an infinite one.

---

[22] Hesiod in *Cosmogony* also conceived of a geocentric universe where the Earth does not move. "Chasm it was, in truth, who was the very first; she soon was followed by broad-breasted Earth, the eternal ground of all" (§115). The chasm is the void. We can contrast from footnote 219 about Lurianic Kabbalah where it is light that exists primordially, not the void.

[23] Ironically, there is a proof by Newton that ends in the absurd conclusion that all orbits must be circular. It is criticized by Hegel in his dissertation, *Dissertation on the Orbits of the Planets*, where he states (Section 1), "Newton's proof in fact shows that both the arcs and the areas are proportional to time whereas the intention was to prove that definitely not the arcs, but only the areas are proportional to time."

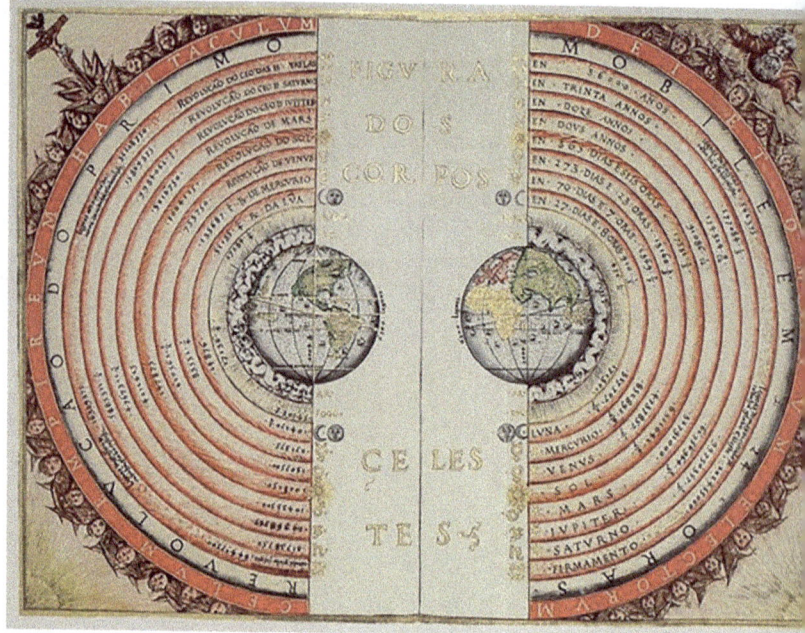

Figure 3: Ptolemy's Model of the Universe

Anaximander's conception of the open universe is one that is *apeiron*, boundless or without limit[24]. This would describe the act of the universe infinitely expanding[25], while it would not describe the universe's calculable and

---

[24] Anaximander, DK12B1

[25] Max Tegmark, *Our Mathematical Universe*, p. 144:

"1. In almost all parts of space, inflation will eventually end in a Big Bang like ours.

2. There will nonetheless be some points in space where inflation never ends.

finite size at each frozen point in time[26]. We cannot say that the universe is infinitely large currently, but we can say it is *potentially* so, as it is increasing with infinite progress, although not at an infinite rate or constant.

The Heisenberg Uncertainty Principle de-centers human notions about measurement and ontology[27]. In quantum physics the sheer act of measurement affects the nature in which a particle passes through a slit[28].

---

3. The total inflating volume increases forever, doubling at regular intervals.
4. The total post-inflationary volume containing galaxies also increases forever, doubling at regular intervals.

[26] Hawking and Penrose, *The Nature of Space and Time*, p. 78: "In cosmology one is interested in measurements that are made in a finite region, rather than at infinity. We are on the inside of the universe, not looking in from the outside." They also state in *The Nature of Space and Time*, p. 98: "The no-boundary proposal implies that the universe is spatially closed. A closed universe will collapse again before an observer has time to see all the universe."

[27] Werner Heisenberg, *Physics and Philosophy*, §3: "What we observe is not nature herself, but nature exposed to our method of questioning."

[28] According to the Heisenberg Uncertainty Principle, it is impossible to know both the position and velocity of a photon particle at once. When the light passes through two slits at once, it is a wave. When it is going through only one slit, it is a particle. Observation or measurement freezes the photon particle's movement through one slit and prevents it from being changed to a wave. Quantum mechanics is just the uncertainty principle; there is no wave observed because we are trying to know the position of the particle when we already have the velocity. Paul Dirac, *The*

This is because human consciousness is a physically detectable quantum energy that in the act of observation or measurement, interacts with the energy of the wave in the experiment to render it a photon. A wave is a photon in movement. *As quantum energy, consciousness directed at a wave collapses the wave function* or motion of the wave to a stationary particle by repelling gravity and slowing down time, akin to a black hole which is composed of dark energy. The effect that consciousness's dark energy has upon a wave in rendering it into a photon can be described by the equation $d*a$, where d is the degree to which time slows down in the presence of dark energy, and a is the surface area of the wave. A photon is a particle of negligible mass, which means it is dispersed by the wave function.

It is said that if time were to stop, we would not see anything because it would also stop the travel of photons from reaching our eye. Likewise, the dilation of time will disperse the wave into an individual photon. This is my attempt at solving the problem of why a wave of light turns into a photon by the effect of consciousness being present when measured.

Principles of Quantum Mechanics, p. 4: "If a system is [quantum-level] small, we cannot observe it without producing a serious disturbance and hence we cannot expect to find any causal connexion between the results of our observations"

The way in which light passes through two slits simultaneously when not measured indicates Bohr's ontological complementarity; a particle can be a particle or wave depending on its movement,[29] as it only manifests to the human eye as one of these when we know the particle's position, and a wave cannot be observed when the photon's activity is tracked. Hence, trying to make man's observation the anchor of scientific activity is unsuccessful[30],[31], but we do know that at the center of quantum activity is its determining factor of consciousness. We can further deduce that consciousness is dark energy

---

[29] *Atom and Archetype,* p. xxxix: "Wave and particle are in constant juxtaposition, though only one can be perceived and measured at one time. In this comparison, the movements of the unconscious into consciousness are like waves of psyche manifesting at nodal points as particles of consciousness."

[30] Arkady Plotnitsky: *Complementarity: Anti-Epistemology after Bohr and Derrida,* p. 3: "As shall be seen, Derrida himself sees his theoretical work expressly in terms of undecidability rather than, and in opposition to, indeterminacy. In this sense-and in the second sense of the word "after" -the anti-epistemology of this study is more after Bohr than after Derrida."

[31] Deleuze and Guattari, *What is Philosophy,* p. 129: "As a general rule, the observer is neither inadequate nor subjective: even in quantum physics, Heisenberg's demon does not express the impossibility of measuring both the speed [more accurately, momentum] and the position of a particle on the grounds of a subjective interference of the measure with the measured, but it measures exactly an objective state of affairs."

because of the causal effect it has on light's form in the absence of mass or spatial extent. There is an objectively extant level of activity at the quantum level that remains unobserved when we try to measure it, showing how the physical world is shaped by conscious activity[32]. We don't know if the universe is fundamentally particle or wave, which is why we assume duality,

---

[32] Robert Lanza, *Biocentrism*, p. 81: "When quantum theory implies that consciousness must exist, it tacitly shows that the content of the mind is the ultimate reality, and that only an act of observation can confer shape and form to reality— from a dandelion in a meadow to sun, wind, and rain"

in the theory of Bohr[33]. The Heisenberg Uncertainty Principle[34], also has radical definitions for the theory of materialism and what it means to be a

---

[33] Arkady Plotnitsky, *Chaosmologies,* p. 47: "Bohr, too, stresses the objective character of all quantum mechanical observation and phenomena, and one can only speak of a 'limit of knowledge', in the sense that no knowledge of the kind classical mechanics offers as concerns its objects is available". Michael Epperson, *Quantum Physics and the Philosophy of Alfred North Whitehead,* ix, states: "Quantum mechanics seems to entail two competing and incompatible fundamental descriptions of nature, and this leaves one with three alternatives: (i) to characterize nature as fundamentally particulate wherein wave-like properties are an abstraction; (ii) to characterize nature as fundamentally wave-like wherein particulate properties are an abstraction; (iii) to pass through these two horns and deny that nature is capable of fundamental characterization at all (apart from this sanction itself, of course) such that we merely characterize our complementary *experiences* of nature as wave-like or particle-like depending on the circumstances, rather than characterizing nature herself. To each of these viewpoints we can associate various theorists--Einstein, for example, to the first, Schrödinger to the second, Bohr to the third, and so forth". Alfred North Whitehead, *Process and Reality,* p. 36, remarks: "The proper balance between atomism and continuity is of importance to physical science. For example, the doctrine, here explained, conciliates Newton's corpuscular theory of light with the wave theory."

[34] $q*p* \sim= h$, where h is Planck's constant, and * designates the degree of imprecision of measurement. Beverley Zabriskie, *Atom and Archetype,* p. xxiv: Formulated by Heisenberg in 1927, "the product of the measurement uncertainty of two complementary observables cannot be smaller than h/4 pi, where h is the Planck constant."

particle[35]. If the universe is fundamentally a wave, it is at its most basic level diaphanous light weaving through space, as Schrödinger believed. This is in contrast to the view that the fundamental unit of matter is still a photon particle that can take on waveform at times[36]. "Bohr's complementarity gives a more radical interpretation to the uncertainty relations. This interpretation prohibits even an assignment or unambiguous definition of physical properties, such as a position or a momentum, to quantum objects and behaviour, rather than only establishing the limit (defined by Planck's

---

[35] David Bohm, *Wholeness and the Implicate Order*, p. 196: "In any case, the wave-particle properties of matter show that the overall movement depends on the total experimental arrangement in a way that is not consistent with the idea of autonomous motion of localized particles; and, of course, the discussion of the Heisenberg microscope experiment indicates the relevance of a new order of undivided wholeness in which it has no meaning to talk about an observed object as if it were separate from the entire experimental situation in which observation takes place. So the use of the descriptive term 'particle' in this 'quantum' context is very misleading."

[36] Alfred North Whitehead, *Process and Reality*, p. 36: "A corpuscle is in fact an 'enduring object.' The notion of an 'enduring object' is, however, capable of more or less completeness of realization. Thus, in different stages of its career, a wave of light may be more or less corpuscular." We can consider this true, since a photon is a particle of negligible mass, and a wave is a dispersed photon.

constant, h) upon the degree of precision with which both can be simultaneously measured."[37]

---

[37] Arkady Plotnitsky, *Chaosmologies*, p. 46

III. Panenpsychism

We might define consciousness as the activity of quantum energy waves in organisms that is present throughout the universe. Relevant to the energy form of consciousness, I will discuss the nature of panenpsychism[38], of consciousness as a concentrated form of energy or "soul" able to permeate the entire universe in a state of Brahman, while matter is energy in condensed, reconstituted form. That is to say that the energy or electrons of consciousness are *potentially* in everything (pan*en*psychism) and that the activity of consciousness includes all things in the fabric of space-time in some parallel dimension, although in actuality consciousness is not in all things; hence the use of the term pan*en*psychism rather than panpsychism[39]. Consciously alive beings obviously have an *aenergic* quality to them that is more complex than that of inert objects such as rocks or stardust.

---

[38] In the word panentheism, *en* is used to denote the fact that God is in the universe, as opposed to pantheism, where God is everywhere in the universe. Hence, I have used panenpsychism to denote the fact that psyche is in the universe as Leibnizian monads, although it is not everywhere.

[39] Deleuze and Guattari, *What is Philosophy,* p. 213: "Vitalism has always had two possible interpretations: that of an Idea that acts, but is not-that acts therefore only from the point of view of an external cerebral knowledge (from Kant to Claude Bernard); or that of a force that is but does not act-that is therefore a pure internal Awareness (from Leibniz to Ruyer)."

The behavior of energy in the world, including consciousness, conforms to what is harmonic or anharmonic. This binary of (an/)harmonism describes the behavior of sound as well as light. While (an/)harmonic can be used to describe measurable activity at the quantum level[40], harmony or disharmony describes activity at the macro level, such as that of planets in motion[41] orbiting around stars. Harmony refers to the functioning or operation of activity of elements in a predictable manner, according to regular and orderly laws or a symmetrical or parallel structure. It is a concept that is found in Gottfried Leibniz (i.e. as pre-established harmony[42]) in addition to Johann Wolfgang von Goethe's cosmology[43].

---

[40] Beverley Zabriskie, *Atom and Archetype,* p. xxxv:: "Pauli's insight was 'that, at the quantum level, all of nature engages in an abstract dance' and is divided into two groups, 'according to whether they engage in an anti symmetric or a symmetric dance'. ... His 'notions of symmetry within the quantum domain' explain why particles with the same energy are always apart from each other. 'This exclusion of particles from each other's energy space ... arises out of ... the abstract movement of the particles as a whole.'"
[41] Goethe, *Faust,* Prologue: pg. 7: Raphael: "The Sun intones, in ancient journey with brother-spheres, a rival song, fulfilling its predestined journey"
[42] Leibniz, Letter to Arnaud, 1686. See Chapter 3, page 77 on pre-established harmony
[43] See page 78 on Goethe's cosmology in Faust.

Chapter Two. Cosmophenomenology

I. Lifeworld and Givenness

It is worth noting what Edmund Husserl, father of phenomenology, referred to as *Lebenswelt* or lifeworld in his writings. Lifeworld denotes the subjective ability to experience feeling, thoughts, intuition, and other cognitive functions from the standpoint of the "I"[44]. It provides an epistemological method of givenness, where we trust the experience of the neurotypical "I" to

---

[44] Husserl, Edmund. 1954 (1970). *The Crisis of European Sciences and Transcendental Phenomenology*. Evanston: Northwestern University Press. pp. 127–128: "The lifeworld is a realm of original self-evidences. That which is self-evidently given is, in perception, experienced as 'the thing itself', in immediate presence, or, in memory, remembered as the thing itself ... [It is] the world of straightforward intersubjective experiences ... all the built-up levels of validity acquired by men for the world of their common life. [It is experienced] ... primarily through seeing, hearing etc., and ... other modes of the ego ... Thus we are concretely in the field of perception ... and in the field of consciousness ... through our living body, but not only in this way, [also] as full ego-subjects ... [W]e, each 'I-the-man' and all of us together, belong to the world as living with one another in the world, valid for our consciousness as existing precisely through this 'living together'. We, as living in wakeful world-consciousness, are constantly active on the basis of our passive having of the world; it is from there, by objects pre given in our consciousness, that we are affected; it is to this or that object that we pay attention, according to our interests; with them we deal actively in different ways; through our acts they are thematic objects ..."

be valid[45]. Inasmuch as lifeworld is experience from a first-person point of view, it is inextricably bound up with that of consciousness and the full capacity of conscious perceptions, thoughts, feelings, and range of experience while we wrongly negate the validity of the range of experiences of common near-death occurrences and out-of-body experiences deemed para-phenomenological.

To accept consciousness as a constant[46] in the universe is to also embrace the lifeworld that is attached with it, including the ability to perceive, remember, and feel emotions for the eternity that consciousness is a reality[47]. To trust in givenness is also to embrace descriptions of alterity and be open to experiences that are not typical to the range of our everyday events and lives or what we perceive to be the horizon of our "I". It is why cosmophenomenology can better supplement traditional approaches of givenness. In other words, while phenomenology is self-referential, cosmophenomenology can lead to a more expansive study of consciousness

---

[45] Jean-Luc Marion, *In Excess*, p. 11: "It is seen immediately that this transfer to and this refoundation of primacy on the noetic authority alone themselves rely entirely on the primacy of the "I".

[46] T.M. Knox, *Aesthetics*, p. xi: "Everything in nature is finite, bounded by something else. But spirit is infinite"

[47] Leibniz, *Monadology*, §21: "For it cannot perish, nor can it subsist without some affection, which is nothing other than its perception."

because it does not limit itself to perception within the horizon of the "I". It can lead to a wider horizon of collective consciousness and consciousness from the standpoint of quantum physics (quantum consciousness).

Daniel Dennett in *Consciousness Explained* has sidestepped the hard problem of consciousness for almost the entirety of the book. Instead, he has stated that consciousness is a mystery, only briefly, in passing[48]. This superficial exploration of the phenomenon is one I believe can be supplemented by the Orch-OR theory of Penrose and Hameroff.

Describing the hard problems of consciousness, David Chalmers, one of the Dennett detractors, characterizes them as "explaining the following phenomena: the ability to discriminate, categorize, and react to environmental stimuli, the integration of information by a cognitive system, the reportability of mental states, the ability of a system to access its own internal states, the focus of attention, the deliberate control of behavior, and the difference between wakefulness and sleep"[49]. According to Chalmers, the truly hard problem of consciousness is that of subjective experience, which we have labelled the lifeworld, Husserl's term.

---

[48] Daniel Dennett, *Consciousness Explained*, p. 255: "Consciousness is still a mystery"
[49] Chalmers, "The Hard Problem of Consciousness" in the Blackwell *Companion to Consciousness*, p. 225

The essence of consciousness is that it is self-referential. A conscious being has awareness of itself being conscious. An organism with higher-order consciousness has self-awareness, i.e. knows that it is alive. The electrons of this energy-consciousness are being entangled at the quantum level with the consciousness of other beings. Thus, the collective nature of consciousness (Hegel's Spirit) is also worth mentioning.

The essence of consciousness is that of a fractal[50]. Self-reference or self-awareness[51] is an inherent feature of higher-order or high-grade consciousness. The structure and nature of consciousness is best geometrically depicted as a fractal[52] (Fig. 1) because like a fractal, a

---

[50] Stuart Hameroff and Deepak Chopra, "The "Quantum Soul": A Scientific Hypothesis" , p. 5: "Penrose suggests such Platonic values, along with precursors of physical laws, constants, forces, and consciousness, literally exist as patterns in fundamental space-time, encoded in Planck scale geometry"

[51] T.M. Knox, *Aesthetics,* p. x:" The eye does not see itself except through its reflection in a mirror. Consciousness becomes aware of itself by being aware of objects and then by being reflected back into itself from them."

[52] Valtteri Arstila and Dan Lloyd, *Subjective Time,* p. 95: "It is consistent with Husserl's indication that "it pertains to the essence of conscious life to contain an intentional intertwining, motivation and mutual implication by meaning," although whether it does so "in a way which in its form and principle has no analogue at all to the physical" is an issue that we set aside here." (1977, 26). The image of the fractal: the structure of the living present the now phase of consciousness--its protention,

consciousness turns in on itself and it simultaneously interacts (tessellates) with other consciousnesses, infinitesimally and infinitely. Fractals are literal veilings/constrictions/condensations of TzimTzum, or spiralling primordial divine light as consciousness (cf. footnote 222).

Because space is not absolute, there is no limit to the number of microcosms within an amount of space, or macrocosms it is part of. This applies to the structure of Gilles Deleuze's metaphysics of the fold (*pli*) which is further discussed in Chapter VIII in relation to memory. This loop or spiral is the activity of quantum entangled photons of the brain, which other than collective consciousness could account for something as basic to individual consciousness as memory, which will further be discussed in the subsequent chapters[53].

---

primal intention, retention. But every element also reflects this structure again-- primal impression by itself is an abstraction, but to think it in this structure is to think it with (or having) this structure, primal impression in its intentional functioning, reflects the retentional and protentional components, and vice versa.
[53] *New Scientist, January* 2010.

Figure 1: Fractal Geometry

In Chapter One, I had described the potentially infinite expansion of the cosmos while criticizing materialism's circularity. So instead of traditional physics alone, I am going to utilize cosmophenomenology, a combination of cosmological physics and phenomenology. Cosmophenomenology, a term first coined by the Danish theologian and philosopher K.E. Løgstrup[54], describes an approach that extends traditional phenomenology to include the relation between human beings and reality as a whole (including nature), from a point of view of the universe, rather than simply human-to-human relations. As such, it extends beyond anthropocentric and speciesist views of consciousness. I am using cosmophenomenology to discuss the necessary relations between consciousness and dark energy, quantum mechanics, alterity, harmony, and

---

[54] *Origin and Surrounding, Metaphysics III*

multiple worlds in this and subsequent chapters. We cannot study the ontology of consciousness with the limitations of phenomenology or cosmological physics alone. Cosmophenomenology is a combination of the two.

II. The Constant of Consciousness

The bulk of this book involves the metaphysics of consciousness. **Consciousness is not ordinary matter, but rather, a polymorphous type of quantum dark energy that has not yet been categorized.** I directly refute Max Tegmark's view that consciousness is a type of ordinary matter[55]. Physicists consider vacuum energy or dark energy to be the cosmological constant[56]. Robert Lanza considers consciousness to be the cosmological constant[57]. I say, they are the same. It is dark energy that, in addition to creating and dictating more space between matter and time by causing its relativity, is a crucial force of sentient and sapient life.

We take the meaning of "dark" in dark matter and dark energy to mean something akin to "alternate forms detected by the absence of matter or energy" (my wording). I conjecture that consciousness, expressible as biophotons[58] of ultraweak light, is a type of dark energy that can directly

---

[55] Cf. Max Tegmark's theorizing of consciousness as "perceptonium", a new type of matter that is ordinary. ("Consciousness as a State of Matter, 2015")

[56] Raphael Bousso, "The Cosmological Constant Problem, Dark Energy, and the Landscape of String Theory"

[57] Cf. *Biocentrism* by Robert Lanza, and Chapter IX. of this thesis on the subject.

[58] Popp, Fritz-Albert, et. al, "Biophoton emission. New evidence for coherence and DNA as source," p. 33.

convert itself to light by reverting between waves and quantum photon particles, as with all light observed in the quantum slit experiment[59]. It was shown that ultraweak photon emission from the surface of human skin was emitted into the visual and infrared spectrum and is strongly correlated to electrodermal activity. Human beings are, in some sense, fundamentally beings of light. The dark energy of the soul or consciousness is expressible as biophotons, like spectral energy in ghosts. Biophoton particles, like regular photons[60], interchange their form with that of the light wave. Consciousness has been shown to abide by the wave function, and display quantum activity, fluctuating between biophotons in *atman* and wave in entangled form of these biophotons, *Brahman* (my Sanskrit characterizations).

While the validity of space and time as constructs can be disproven with Einstein's theory of relativity, that would leave consciousness to be the sole

---

[59] *Perhaps all light is dark* (no pun intended). Photons have been shown to interact with fields and forces to have an effect that is similar to dark energy repelling space. Cf. Kouwn et al, "Massive photon and dark energy"

[60] Popp, "Properties of Biophotons and their Theoretical Implications," p. 393: "The total intensity (i) from a few up to some hundred photons indicates that the phenomenon is quantum physical, since fewer than about 100 photons are ever present in the photon field under investigation."

ontological constant of the universe[61],[62],[63] because it can exist in a vacuum, also called a plenum or void. Black holes are dark energy that absorbs all else (except, of course, dark energy, which is the only thing that survives them). Consciousness as dark energy is not dependent upon ordinary matter or dark matter to survive[64], but rather subsumes all matter.

Bergson has in turn attempted to refute Einstein with his view of the *durée,* a concept of time measured in terms of conscious perception rather than by objective units of time[65]. The *durée* holds a surprising validity, as

---

[61] Robert Lanza, *Biocentrism,* p. 189: "Because consciousness transcends the body, ... we're left with Being or consciousness as the bedrock components of existence"

[62] Robert Lanza, *Biocentrism,* p. 188: "Robert Lanza, *Biocentrism,* p. 188: "The biocentric view of the timeless, spaceless cosmos of consciousness allows for no true death in any real sense."

[63] Penrose, *Shadows of the Mind,* p. 409: "It would hardly be helpful to imagine oneself to 'be' an automaton, since an automaton--by definition *unconscious*--is not something that is possible to be at all!

[64] T. M. Knox, *Aesthetics,* p. xi: "Everything in nature is finite, bounded by something else. But spirit is infinite"

[65] Bergson, *Duration and Simultaneity,* p. 45: "How do we pass from this inner time to the time of things? We perceive the physical world and this perception appears, rightly or wrongly, to be inside and outside us at one and the same time; in one way, it is a state of consciousness; in another, a surface film of matter in which perceiver and perceived coincide. To each moment of our inner life there thus corresponds a

consciousness is dark energy which affects the constitution or consistency of spacetime. The ontological constancy (fundamental) of consciousness would mean that consciousness would also survive death in some form.

The survival of consciousness beyond death cannot be explained by classical physics which is applicable to ordinary matter, but rather only by quantum physics[66] which regards the energy fields underlying atoms. The very phenomena of quantum physics repudiates ordinary materialism and physicalism which are dependent upon classical physics. The move of a materialist would be to extend the very position of materialism to physicalism, or to exaggerate the definition of "matter" to dark energy and dark matter, although it has been explained that neither move will be coherent (see Chapter I, Section I). In the theory of Hameroff and Penrose, where consciousness occurs as the quantum activity in microtubules within neurons, the basic

---

moment of our body and of all surrounding matter that is "simultaneous" with it; this matter then seems to participate in our conscious duration."

[66] *Atom and Archetype*, p. xviii. "Twentieth-century physics, dealing with the atomic and subatomic phenomena that cannot be apprehended by everyday intuition and thus necessitate the introduction of new concepts such as energy quanta and the fundamental uncertainty of measured values. A quantum is an indivisible, discrete entity of a physical quantity such .. energy, which in earlier physics was regarded as continuous."

framework for the soul or consciousness constituting quantum information would survive upon death[67]. Microtubules are 25 nanometers in diameter, and vary in length[68]. If the soul is quantum information outside the microtubules, then we could say that the soul exists most obviously in death, where there is duality between the soul and the body[69]. In life, in *atman,* there is monism

---

[67] Stuart Hameroff, *Through the Wormhole* documentary, "Let's say the heart stops beating, the blood stops flowing; the micro-tubules lose their quantum state. The quantum information within the microtubules is not destroyed, it can't be killed, and it just distributes and dissipates to the universe at large. If the patient is resuscitated, revived, this quantum information can go back into the microtubules, and the patient says 'I had a near-death experience.' If they're not revived, and the patient dies, it's possible that this quantum information can exist outside the body, perhaps indefinitely, as a soul." We can compare this quantum information to "solitons" which are quasiparticles that remain in waveform perpetually. This is the form that quasiparticles take in entanglement

[68] Hameroff and Penrose, "Consciousness in the Universe"

[69] Laibl Wolf, Practical Kabbalah: "The most profound disintegration of the soul-body duality occurs at death. Here the dislocation of the soul from the body is so intense that only a tenuous relationship is maintained. But Kabbalah teaches that even in death a basic level of integration still exists, and the body retains its physical form. The body's progressive decay is really the loosening of this final bond ... Recordings of near death experiences have provided us with a window into the nature of the soul-body duality. In certain ways the near death phenomenon is similar to some meditative states and out-of-body experiences described in Kabbalistic literature."

between body and soul. However, the fact that the dark energy of consciousness affects matter and material processes and is expressible as matter and light, does not mean it is identical to matter or light. The photons of consciousness that are quantum-entangled display behavior that is darkly aenergic by becoming wave because dark energy is its origin.

We can speak of will/life as directive force for both Schopenhauer[70] and Nietzsche[71]: *prana* in Sanskrit. The equivalent of this for Bergson would be the

---

[70] Schopenhauer, *The World as Will and Representation,* pg. 403: "The whole body is the visible expression of the will to live, yet the motives corresponding to this will no longer act, indeed the dissolution of the body, the end of the individual, and thus the greatest suppression of the natural will, is welcome and desired."

[71] In Nietzsche we can speak both of a will to power (pg. 400: "Thus in the history of morality a will to power finds expression") and a will to life (pg. 401: "The will to nothingness has become master over the will to life!") The difference between Schopenhauer and Nietzsche is in the belief that one must learn a passive resignation or diminished will to life from tragedy. Nietzsche in the *Will to Power* states p. 23, "suffering might predominate, and in spite of that a powerful will might exist, a Yes to life, a need for this predominance."

elan vital[72], or the *qi* in Chinese thought, and the libido[73] in Jung, all energy. Everything in the universe is an expression of energy[74], whether or not the thing that is expressing energy is alive or not; and all the more so for beings that are alive. Prana is Spirit or Schopenhauerian will, that is, consciousness or intentionality in the matter throughout the Universe.

The panpsychists believe that everything in the Universe has an ounce of

---

[72] Bergson, too, distinguishes things in terms of being willed or inert: *Creative Evolution,* p. 236: "Vital is in the direction of the voluntary. We may say then that this first kind of order is that of the vital or of the willed, in opposition to the second, which is that of the inert and the automatic."

[73] Jung, *Atom and Archetype,* p. xxxii, "In physics, too, we speak of energy and its various manifestations... the situation in psychology is precisely the same ..•. We are dealing primarily with energy, with measures of intensity, with greater or lesser quantities ... in various guises. If we conceive of libid.o as energy, we can take a comprehensive and unified view ... such as is provided in the physical sciences by the theory of energetics .... I see man's drives as various manifestations of energic processes ... forces analogous to heat, light, etc"

[74] Henri Bergson, *Matter and Memory*, p. 235: "No doubt also the material universe itself, defined as the totality of images, is a kind of consciousness, a consciousness in which everything compensates and neutralizes everything else, a consciousness of which all the potential parts, balancing each other by a reaction which is always equal to the action, reciprocally hinder each other from standing out." We can say, then, that the universe as well as consciousness functions according to a type of harmony, where the whole is a sum of parts operating together and in accordance with laws.

psyche, vitality, sub-mind, Spirit or prana. However, they can be refuted by saying that not all energy or matter contains prana; see inert objects such as rocks, for example. This is why we previously referred to panenpsychism. We can, however, turn to the quantum electrodynamic equation $E=MC^2$: Matter as a form of condensed energy is directly proportional in form to the nature of the energy of which it is condensed and arises out of. Dark energy produces dark matter, and more ordinary light energy produces ordinary matter, although it is possible for dark energy, the most primordial and ubiquitous stuff in the universe, to interact with ordinary matter and ordinary light (ordinary light has displayed quantum activity that is dark, see Kouwn et al, "Massive photon and dark energy").

The First Law of Thermodynamics or Julius Robert Mayer's law of the conservation of energy states that energy can only change form but never be destroyed or come into being. If energy is imperishable, so, too, is matter, which is energy in condensed form[75].

---

[75] Robert Lanza, *Biocentrism*, p. 191, "Because absolutely everything has an energy-identity, nothing is exempt from this immortality".
William Huggins as quoted by Carl Sagan in *Cosmos*, p. 18: "A community of matter appears to exist throughout the visible universe, for the stars contain many of the elements which exist in the Sun and Earth. It is remarkable that the elements most widely diffused through the host of stars are some of those most

The premise of this book is the following. Consciousness as energy never goes out of Being (as proven by the mathematical equations of physics and by thousands of direct phenomenological testimonies regarding near-death experiences following resuscitation from a state of physical death)[76]. Energy is neither created nor destroyed; it can only be changed from one form to another[77]. Once we die, although our bodies are decaying, our consciousness lives on in a different form, via an intact frame of quantum information once inside the microtubules the energy hid in. The energy is then released into the universe, becoming one with a higher parallel dimension in which greater

---

closely connected with the living organisms of our globe, including hydrogen, sodium, magnesium, and iron. May it not be that, at least, the brighter stars are like our Sun, the upholding and energizing centres of systems of worlds, adapted to be the abode of living beings?".
Anaxagoras, Cosmological Fragments, p. 17: "The Hellenes follow a wrong usage in speaking of coming into being and passing away; for nothing comes into being or passes away, but there is mingling and separation of things that are. So they would be right to call coming into being mixture, and passing away separation."

[76] Long and Perry, *Evidence of the Afterlife,* p. 57: Among those having a cardiac arrest, about 10 to 20 percent will have a near-death experience.

[77] $E=MC2$ coupled with the First Law of Thermodynamics or Julius Robert Mayer's law of the conservation of energy states that energy only changes form but cannot be destroyed. It can be seen as a version of Anaxagoras's statement that nothing comes into being nor goes out of being. This would logically include consciousness.

objects of consciousness can be accessed. That is not to say that the biophotons of consciousness are scattered inaccessibly or irretrievably to constitute the soul as an unrecognizable entity. They are indeed still in an intact state, but in the higher dimension, the consciousness is at one with all things in wave-state because they are not confined to microtubules and can potentially be entangled with anything. It is this type of omnipresence that we call "Brahman": the fundamental unification of all consciousnesses or life-energies in the universe.

Consciousness is one form of dark energy dispersed to different degrees, in life and in death as ordinary light, and located between atoms or in matter itself. The entire Universe is fundamentally composed of energy, which takes upon one of two forms: pure and saturated like energy, or condensed and dispersed like matter. Dark energy is dynamic and virtually omnipresent, or mutable, as the Deleuzian multiplicity. The dispersed form is what we may call Deleuzian multiplicity in quantum entanglement emerging and changing of qualities of energy even in the *atman* state[78].

---

[78] Tegmark, "Consciousness as a State of Matter," p. 3: "Just as there are many types of liquids, there are many types of consciousness."

III. Quantum Entanglement

Consciousness is typically defined to be the quantum activity inside brain neuron microtubules. This activity, I contend, is a micro-dark energy which does not obey the typical laws of matter as it is not confined to space nor time. The quantum entanglement of the electrons of two or more beings across space[79] interacting shows that the energy of consciousness does not obey the typical laws of matter. In quantum entanglement, there can be inter-conscious interaction, whether it is intentional or not. In quantum non-locality, particles can instantly teleport across large distances, as in a plenum or null space[80]. String theory posits that all matter, at the fundamental or root level, is

---

[79] Alfred North Whitehead, *Process and Reality*, p. 36: "For both a corpuscle, and an advancing element of at wave front, are merely a permanent form propagated from atomic creature to atomic creature."

[80] Leibniz, *Monadology*, §61: "For the whole is a plenum, which makes all matter interconnected, and in a plenum every movement has some effect on distant bodies in proportion to their distance, such that each body is affected not only by those which touch it, and in some way feels the effect of everything that happens to them, but also by means of them it is affected by those which touch the former ones, the ones which directly touch it. From this it follows that this communication extends indefinitely. Consequently every body is affected by everything that happens in the universe, so much so that the one who sees all could read in each body what is happening everywhere, and even what has happened or will happen, by observing in the present that which is remote both in time and space"

interconnected. This would make quantum entanglement seem more plausible because photons are traveling in a pre-existing material or aenergic path. Spatial quantum entanglement, i.e. the entwining of two beings' consciousness or electrons throughout space can be random, and demonstrates that space does not exist in its traditional sense or impede entanglement, as distance does not make any difference in quantum entanglement occurring. Hence, the behavior of photons of consciousness can be said to be non-local, or in the case of interconnected particles in string theory, atypically local.

Quantum entanglement further demonstrates the nonexistence or non-validity of space. In order for quantum entanglement to occur, two beings' quantum activity or consciousness must be at the same level or frequency. Then, its interaction can be harmonic. This is a harmonic activity of the anharmonic activity of consciousness, where music is being made despite the anharmonic perturbations, or out of anharmonic rhythms.

A. Time

Consciousness throughout time can also be entangled. **Dark matter is neither confined by ordinary space nor time.** *If we view spacetime as a fabric of constructs, it is possible for consciousness to traverse it.* It would further demonstrate that time is not linear and could possibly be simultaneously accessed. Hence, I might somehow be able to see myself in a vision or dream that is claircognizant and accurate, months or days before the incident in question occurs. Entanglement would also explain premonition, where the Mind is entangled with reality from access to a dimension in which spacetime can be simultaneously perceived.

B. Space

It has been stated that consciousness is a unique type of undiscovered dark energy expressible as biophotons. We can liken consciousness to the type of energy-matter duality seen in the quantum slit experiment. At first glance, consciousness seems enmattered in only its photon particle form. However when a person glances at the particle, imbuing a focused and direct stream of energy, the nanoparticles of the atom in question seem morphed into wave form. This possibly shows that all light is a form of dark energy that morphs between two forms. It is as if matter "knows" it is being watched since it is dependent upon the presence of consciousness--perhaps a fellow form of dark energy. Given the condition of this being watched, precision regarding observation of the particle's activity as wave is impossible; the presence of the human eye or act of watching the photon's velocity facilitates the photon only appearing as a stationary particle because we cannot know its location simultaneously. Hence, we might say that matter is a polymorphous duality of particle (matter) with wave (energy) potentiality, where a photon is in two states at once. It is wave energy that facilitates the travel of photons in the act of local entanglement or dark energy quantum activity. Quantum entanglement of two objects would occur when their energy auras or photon shells are in contact[81], as well as for two objects whose auras are well spaced apart and not in contact.

C. Synchronicity

Synchronicity is the co-occurrence between a mental event and an event occurring in the external or physical world[82]. Carl Jung has defined it as "an acausal connecting principle," "acausal parallelism" and "meaningful

---

[81] Jeffrey S. Keen, "Entanglement of Large-Sized Objects, p. 1: " short-range entanglement naturally occurs for any 2 large bodies when their auras are in contact. In this case, a complex pattern of subtle energies is produced and involves the 2 bodies being linked by different subtle energy and properties"

[82] *Atom and Archetype,* p. xviii: "Jung's term for phenomena that coincide in time and space for which there is no causal explanation but which have a clear meaningful connection. They can occur between psyche and psyche, telepathically to a certain extent, as well as between psyche and physis-i.e., outside, in physical reality (psychokinetically)."

coincidence[83]." Perhaps like the states of energy can be particles or waves the universe as perceived can also be in causal synchronicity or acausal coincidence. It has been previously mentioned how quantum entanglement can connect the minds of two or more people. However, quantum entanglement may also tie mind to matter. Carl Jung describes his own experience with synchronicity:

> "Well, I was sitting opposite [a young woman patient] one day, with my back to the window, listening to her flow of rhetoric. She had an impressive dream the night before, in which someone had given her a golden scarab — a costly piece of jewellery. While she was still telling me this dream, I heard something behind me gently tapping on the window. I turned round and saw that it was a fairly large flying insect that was knocking against the window-pane from outside in the obvious effort to get into the dark room. This seemed to me very strange. I opened the window immediately and caught the insect in the air as it flew in. It was a scarabaeid beetle, or common rose-chafer (*Cetonia aurata*), whose gold-green colour most nearly resembles that of a golden scarab. I handed the beetle to my patient with the words, 'Here is your scarab.'"

---

[83] Carl Jung, *Synchronicity: An Acausal Connecting Principle*

It is up to the reader to determine whether this was a meaningful synchronicity, or simply coincidence that could have a meaning read in without being causal. Here in this instance there may also have been claircognizance, as the patient's dream could have been the prediction of Jung handing the patient the scarab beetle, and the patient interpreting it as jewelry. If the mind is entangled with matter, we can say that the scarab beetle represents matter at a base level. However, we can also say that the limited mind or consciousness of the beetle was also entangled with the mind of the patient at the level of collective consciousness or *Brahman*[84]. The connection between mind and matter is a Gnostic view where matter is designed by the mind, and thus can only be an expression of mind.

The Different Senses of "Mind"

In Korean, the word for mind and heart are synonymous. 마음 [ma-eum] which can also be synonymous for *nous*, can be contrasted from 정신 [jung-shin], the word for sanity, sobriety, right state of mind, or the proper level of "attention" (i.e. in attention-deficit hyperactive disorder)

---

[84] *Atom and Archetype*, p. xix: "The collective unconscious, of which we are really not aware and which mainly manifests itself in archetypal images or situations."

as well as a state of conscious awareness that expresses Heideggerian care or concern about the world.

In German, we can note that *Geist* is translated equally as mind as well as Spirit. Spirit unites minds and spirits in bodies. In Greek, Ψυχή (psyche) is translated as the soul. Plato has noted its immortality[85]. In Korean, the psyche is 영혼 [young-hon], which relates closely to the word 영원 [young-won] or eternal.

The Sanskrit word Brahman represents the universal substance. This is in contrast to Ātman which denotes the embodied Self.

Matter is shown to be condensed and dispersed Mind or Spirit. Matter is a form of tangible energy, like sound is an audible form and light is visible and heat is also tangible. It has also been demonstrated that consciousness is expressible as energy or a series of distinct quantities of biophotons that are quantum entangled in mammalian brains[86].

---

[85] Plato, *Phaedo*, 80b: "The soul is most like the divine, deathless, intelligible, and uniform, indissoluble, always the same in itself."

[86] Popp et. al, 1984. It is not only in brains that this energy is entangled, but it can be entangled across space through/via interpersonal interactions. This fact carries

---

dramatic implications for the materialist strain of traditional analytic philosophy of mind.

IV. A Topology of Selfhood

The grade of Husserlian lifeworld increases with the level of Mind[87] which we can equate with higher-order consciousness in human beings and intelligent mammals such as dolphins and chimpanzees[88]. All grades of consciousness or soul can be deemed manifestations of a mind, but only humans have a mind with rationality, while animals possess sub rationality[89]. The way that animals act is sensory, as Aristotle described[90].

Animals are sentient, possessing at least lower-order consciousness, but

---

[87] Spinoza, *Ethics,* p. 7: "The more reality or being each thing has, the more attributes belong to it."

[88] John Eccles, *Evolution of the Brain, Creation of the Self,* p. 182: " 'We have extremely strong evidence that animals can perform the mental abstraction of the quality of numbers which in human children can only be accomplished by conscious cerebration."

[89] John Eccles, *Evolution of the Brain, Creation of the Self,* p. 182: "Still we must be cautious about identifying these assumed mental states with those humanly experienced. We lack symbolic communication with animals at the subtle level possible between human persons"

[90] Aristotle, De Anima (On the Soul), 429a5-429a8 p. 682: "Because imaginations remain in the organs of sense and resemble sensations, animals in their actions are largely guided by them, some (i.e. the brutes) because of the non-existence in them of thought, others (i.e. men) because of the temporary eclipse in them of thought by feeling or disease or sleep"

only human beings and intelligent mammals are sapient.

Even plants have consciousness, for their auras or photon shells, like those of humans or animals, can be detected electromagnetically[91]. The consciousness of plants does not require a brain, but rather a simple level of pain receptors or basic nervous system[92],[93]. The stronger the consciousness and level of mind's capabilities, it would follow that the strength of the aura and

---

[91] Jeffrey S. Keen, "Communicating with Plants," p. 1, "All objects possess an aura which comprises 7 ellipsoidal shells, whose dimensions are basically static but may vary slowly with changes in the environment 1, 2 such as the phases of the moon, or pressure when squeezed, or the intensity of light, etc. All living things, whether animal or plant, also have an aura, but unlike inert objects, they also possess a Tree of Life 3 and a reacting basic consciousness. The latter allows the size of their auras to be altered rapidly by conscious intent."

[92] Deleuze and Guattari, *What is Philosophy*, p. 212: "Of course, plants and rocks do not possess a nervous system. But, if nerve connections and cerebral integrations presuppose a brainforce as faculty of feeling coexistent with the tissues, it is reasonable to suppose also a faculty of feeling that coexists with embryonic tissues and that appears in the Species as a collective brain; or with the vegetal tissues in the "small species.""

[93] Deleuze and Guattari *What is Philosophy*, p. 213: "Not every organism has a brain, and not all life is organic, but everywhere there are forces that constitute microbrains, or an inorganic life of things."

complexity of mind also grows[94]. Does prana structure itself as a food chain, as matter does? Does more sentient life feed upon less life in embodied physical states due to the existence of matter? It seems that more sapient animals would have more physically complex neurobiological systems. The Darwinistic interpretation of Will to Power in Nietzsche/ fitness[95] states that it is only the fittest who survive, and this so in a predatory fashion. While it is true in the physical sense, that life feeds on life, consciousness, which can be entangled between simple and complex organisms, indicates that life is interdependent in

---

[94] Spinoza, *Ethics,* p. 7: "The more reality or being each thing has, the more attributes belong to it."

[95] R.J. Hollingdale, *Nietzsche, The Man and his Philosophy*, p. 74: "Not only did Nietzsche discover the nature of his dilemma among the Greeks, he also discovered the key to its solution. Long before he had formulated the theory of the will to power he had discovered that the driving force behind the culture of Hellas had been contested, the striving to surpass. . . . The Greeks were cruel, savage, and predatory; yet they had become the most humane people of antiquity, the inventors of philosophy, science and tragedy, the first and finest European nation."

a matrix, to some degree[96],[97],[98].

It has here been mentioned that grades of consciousness differ hierarchically amongst animals and human beings. Humans have the greatest form of consciousness qua creativity and spiritual and aesthetic awareness; that is, they can actively create with their consciousness. Most animals, on the other hand, simply live, very passively, in the environment given to them. This is the animal soul described by Aristotle which operates by senses[99], while Leibniz elaborates that beasts only act according to memory:[100] The latter view

---

[96] See p. 42 on synchronicity

[97] Leibniz, *Monadology*, §51: "But in simple substances, the influence of one monad over another is merely ideal: it can have its effect only through the intervention of God, inasmuch as in the ideas of God a monad rightly demands that God have consideration for it when organising the others from the beginning of things. For since a created monad cannot have a physical influence on the interior of another, this is the only way that one can be dependent on another"

[98] Leibniz, *Monadology*, §56: "Now this interconnection, or this accommodation of all created things to each other and of each to all the rest, means that each simple substance has relations which express all the others, and that consequently it is a perpetual living mirror of the universe"

[99] Aristotle, *De Anima*, II, p. 75: "The first characteristic of an essential animal is sensation"

[100] Leibniz, *The Monadology, 28* "Men act like beasts insofar as the succession of their perceptions is due to the principle of memory alone; they resemble empirical

is the conception agreed upon by Bergson[101]. It is only with a few exceptions, such as dolphins or chimpanzees, who can create tools with fully creative mind-spirit, that we find creative intelligence in animals that is comparable to that of human beings. Sapience (knowing how) is not the same as sentience (knowing that)[102].

Human beings' creative life-force energy is highly concentrated. Animals, it can be said, have a vegetative and animal soul, as Aristotle said, but not a spiritual self-aware level self (rational soul)[103]. Perhaps it is the most sophisticated level of mind in humans that is entrapped in microtubule neuron cells and can survive death via retention of quantum information. This is akin

---

physicians, who have a simple practice without theory. Indeed, in three-quarters of our actions we are nothing but empirics."

[101] Bergson, *Matter and Memory,* p. 82: "When a dog welcomes his master, barking and wagging his tail, he certainly recognizes him; but does this recognition imply the evocation of a past image and the comparison of that image with the present perception? Does it not rather consist in the animal's consciousness of a certain special attitude adopted by his body, an attitude which has been gradually built up by his familiar relations with his master, and which the mere perception of his master now calls forth in him mechanically?"

[102] Robert Brandom, *Making It Explicit: Reasoning, Representing, and Discursive Commitment.*

[103] Aristotle, De Anima (On the Soul), II.1

to the Catholic belief that only humans have a soul or spirit that survives death, while animals do not have a soul.

Only some grades of soul are highly concentrated and linked to a life-force that is aenergic and indestructible. Human consciousness is linked to Brahman in such a way that it can survive and adapt in reincarnation, as Buddhists and Hindus as well as some Jews believe.

B. Higher Order Consciousness/ The Mind

The Mind is a source of consciousness / aenergic will which can be collective (Brahmanic) or individuated (atmic). In a state of of dispersal in quantum entanglement, atmic electrons are quasi-Brahmanic. In a state of death, or during near-death experiences, consciousness is Brahmanic; it has been released from the microtubules that contained it in an atmic state during life and is dissipated at large in the universe[104]. This means that the information

---

[104] Stuart Hameroff, *Through the Wormhole* documentary: ""Let's say the heart stops beating, the blood stops flowing; the micro-tubules lose their quantum state. The quantum information within the microtubules is not destroyed, it can't be killed, and it just distributes and dissipates to the universe at large. If the patient is resuscitated, revived, this quantum information can go back into the microtubules, and the patient says 'I had a near-death experience.' If they're not revived, and the

is disseminated, spread and copied although it does not change in character. As we see in the quantum slit experiment, consciousness as a field of dark energy is a causal force of photons switching to the dark form of the wave. *Light is essentially dark*[105]. In quantum entanglement, the form of dark energy as consciousness can be dispersed into a Deleuzian multiplicity which reflects God (Brahmic quantum entangled Collective Soul) as the source of consciousness and spirit as *collective consciousness.*

It has been shown by the Institute of Noetic Sciences in California[106] that will or intentionality is a form of physically detectable quantum energy. This would support a type of physicalism. In multiple groups of volunteers averaging ten to twelve, it was found that there were distinct perturbations in the wave function[107] based upon the presence of actively meditating people. We can also

---

patient dies, it's possible that this quantum information can exist outside the body, perhaps indefinitely, as a soul."

[105] Pun not intended.

[106] Radin, et. al, "Consciousness and the double-slit interference pattern: Six experiments", 157: " The ratio of the interference pattern's double-slit spectral power to its single-slit spectral power was predicted to decrease when attention was focused toward the double slit as compared to away from it"

[107] Radin, et. al

look at monks practicing *G Tum Mo*[108], a distinct style of yoga in the Himalayan mountains that uses meditation to produce heat in their bodies. Monks envision flames along their spine, which effectively raises body temperature by as much as seventeen degrees Fahrenheit in freezing cold temperatures. Meditation can be used to control homeostatic/basic biological functions and desires such as sexual arousal or biological appetites. Buddhism is about reversing egoistic Darwinist or animal instinct or desire, and cultivating a Higher will that is directly and physically detectible, channeling the mind's willpower (the energy of consciousness) into a causal material force-energy in the world[109]. Will, it can be said, is the most powerful and concentrated form of consciousness or intentionality[110][111]. It is the purest form of energy as the purest form of Spirit

---

[108] Kozhevnikov, Maria, et. al, "Neurocognitive and Somatic Components of Temperature Increases during g-Tummo Meditation: Legend and Reality": G Tum Mo literally means "heat"

[109] Plato, Symposium, 80b: "When soul and body are both in the same place, nature teaches the one to serve and be subject, the other to rule and govern. In this relation which do you think resembles the divine and which is the mortal part? Don't you think that it is the nature of the divine to rule and direct, and that of the mortal to be subject and serve?"

[110] Spinoza, *The Ethics,* p. 28: "Will cannot be called a free cause, but can be called a necessary cause."

[111] Spinoza, *The Ethics,* p. 06: "Will and intellect are one and the same."

or consciousness itself. When concentrated and channeled from the mind toward something, intentionality can be causal. Conscious energy can be creative or destructive, each in productive and nonproductive ways.

Platonic love is tied to Buddhism in that we channel a higher form of Will or Care directed toward a being as a whole, rather than one tied to the Body. Mind love (Agape) is higher than physical love (Eros). It is Agape that touches the will and soul of a person while physical love superficially and only touches the outer edges of a person and is merely symbolic in gesture. According to Agathon, the object of love is beauty[112]. According to the Gnostics, nothing physical can be aesthetically superior or beautiful[113], and so the object of love is all spiritual things, or the soul. In Plato, love can only be love of the eternal

---

[112] Plato, *Symposium,* 199d

[113] In Gnosticism, there is a dualism between what is created and the uncreated eternal Creator God.

Form, and the soul is immortal[114], a view that is also believed by Spinoza[115].

C. Consciousness and the Universe

Both materialism and idealism are simultaneously correct. The quantum slit experiment has shown that matter has its independent way of operating, but can be influenced by the mind at times. Quantum physics, especially the phenomenon of entanglement, has shown that mind and matter are connected. Descartes's doubts[116] were wrong about brains in vats being deceived by God, an evil genius, because it has just been proven that the universe cannot be

---

[114] Plato. Phaedo, 79d: "But when it investigates by itself, it passes into the realm of the pure and everlasting and immortal and changeless, and being of a kindred nature, when it is once independent and free from interference, consorts with it always and strays no longer, but remains, in that realm of the absolute, constant and invariable, through contact with beings of a similar nature. And this condition of the soul we call wisdom"

[115] Benedict de Spinoza, *Ethics:* The human mind cannot be absolutely destroyed with the human body, but there is some part of it which remains eternal.

[116] Descartes, *Meditations*, p. 16: "I shall then suppose, not that God who is supremely good and the fountain of truth, but some evil genius not less powerful than deceitful, has employed his whole energies in deceiving me; I shall consider that the heavens, the earth, colours, figures, sound, and all other external things are nought but the illusions and dreams of which this genius has availed himself in order to lay traps for my credulity"

simulated[117], especially not by a supercomputer. The universe exists in accordance with our interactions and choices. God, if he exists, is not a deceiving supergenius who pulls our strings as if we are marionettes. We also control part of our universe that we perceive with our intentionality, thoughts, and choices.

A Harvard neurosurgeon has written a book about being in a coma he had when brain-dead[118]. This demonstrates that the brain is only minimally tied to consciousness in a purer state that we might attribute to the afterlife. In other words, the brain is only responsible for homeostatic functions. A person can be totally brain-dead, and have a functional Mind. No part of the brain is responsible for our consciousness in totality[119] and the Brain is not ontologically equal to the Mind,[120] but rather, the Mind chooses to utilize the

---

[117] Mcrae, ScienceAlert, September 2017

[118] Eben Alexander, *Proof of Heaven*

[119] Descartes had suggested that the pineal gland accounts for consciousness, something he was wrong about. This is in his earliest biological writings and *The Passions of the Soul, Article 31:* "That there is a little kernel (the pineal gland) in the brain wherein the soul exercises her functions more peculiarly than in the other parts."

[120] John Eccles, *Evolution of the Brain, Creation of the Self,* p. 182: "William James suggested that the mind was a property acquired by a brain that had grown too complex to control itself."

brain for its functional output for an embodied person[121]. It is known that the brain is active after a person is declared dead on the bodily level[122].

The Gnostics believe that the Universe or Cosmos is structured in a topological form, such that the heavens or first-order world is pure energy, as are the beings of light (angels). Humans are also beings of light, although partially, as this is in the form of ultraweak photon emission. Matter is a representation of the Universal Mind (Will) or Greek *Nous*. The Earth created by the Demiurge is impure, tainted, and condensed energy (matter). They were right that matter is a form of tainted or condensed, localized and goopy energy rather than dispersed, omnipresent energy or Spirit.

---

[121] Stuart Hameroff, *Through the Wormhole* documentary: "Let's say the heart stops beating, the blood stops flowing; the micro-tubules lose their quantum state. The quantum information within the microtubules is not destroyed, it can't be killed, and it just distributes and dissipates to the universe at large. If the patient is resuscitated, revived, this quantum information can go back into the microtubules, and the patient says 'I had a near-death experience.' If they're not revived, and the patient dies, it's possible that this quantum information can exist outside the body, perhaps indefinitely, as a soul."

[122] See Chapter 9 and 10 on Pure Consciousness.

The Gnostic view might be related to the Spinozistic and Deistic view of God as an ever-creating force[123]. The first God created the purest heaven, and in turn, this heaven spit out another God, a lesser deity called the Demiurge which created Earth. Christians are worshipping these layers of God as one being.

Some Harvard neuroscientists have concluded that a portion of the brain stem (cortex) is responsible for waking, non-comatose consciousness[124]. It would be the microtubules in this brainstem that would be responsible for waking consciousness, although pure consciousness shows the quantum information inside the microtubules to be released and independently existing from the physical body.

---

[123] Spinoza, *Ethics*, p. 10: "God is the immanent but not the transitive cause of all things." On *Ethics*, p.12, he expounds: "God is the efficient cause, not only of the existence of things, but also of their essence." If God is perfect in essence and existence, it would be expected the things God creates must be perfect, too. But they have imperfect affectations for a reason.

[124] Fisher, David et al, "A human brain network derived from coma-causing brainstem lesions":. "This brainstem site is functionally connected to 2 cortical regions, the AI and pACC, which become disconnected in disorders of consciousness. This network of brain regions may have a role in the maintenance of human consciousness."

A Cosmic Topology

In the Hindu and Buddhist models used in yoga or meditation, the self exists around and centrally focused upon the physical body itself. It exists as a higher self beyond the physical entity, and is composed of six total layers: an etheric body, subtle body, lower and mental body, buddhic body, and atmic body. The atmic body ties the one to the all (Brahman), the collective soul or oversoul. In the higher mental vehicle, the electrons of the monadic spark are dispersed into the universe. The monadic spark explains how electrons become entangled, via quantum entanglement, with that of other people.

Figure 1: A Topology of Self

Chapter Three. Quantum World and Harmony

I. (An/)Harmonics

From the activity of human brain cells to diagrams of light, the wave pattern is fundamental to describing the existence of energy in the universe. As for the harmonic pattern of existence, we can liken it to Western music, such as Bach, whereas anharmonic music is the pattern followed by Indian or Eastern music. The wave pattern can be replicated visually in an oscillator, and sonically in a harmonograph. As mentioned before in Chapter One, all patterns of light or sound in the universe, which are forms of energy, are harmonic or anharmonic.

The pattern of consciousness is anharmonic. It has been said that consciousness defies laws in the universe in terms of its behavior eluding human laws[125]. If we consider harmonics as ordering according to law, then an anharmonic categorization would be deemable as such for consciousness. I will discuss Stuart Hameroff and Roger Penrose's orchestrated objective

---

[125] Robert Lanza, *Biocentrism*, p. 173: "Even the Nobel Laureate physicist Steven Weinberg concedes that there is a problem with consciousness, and that although it may have a neural correlate, its existence does not seem to be derivable from physical laws."

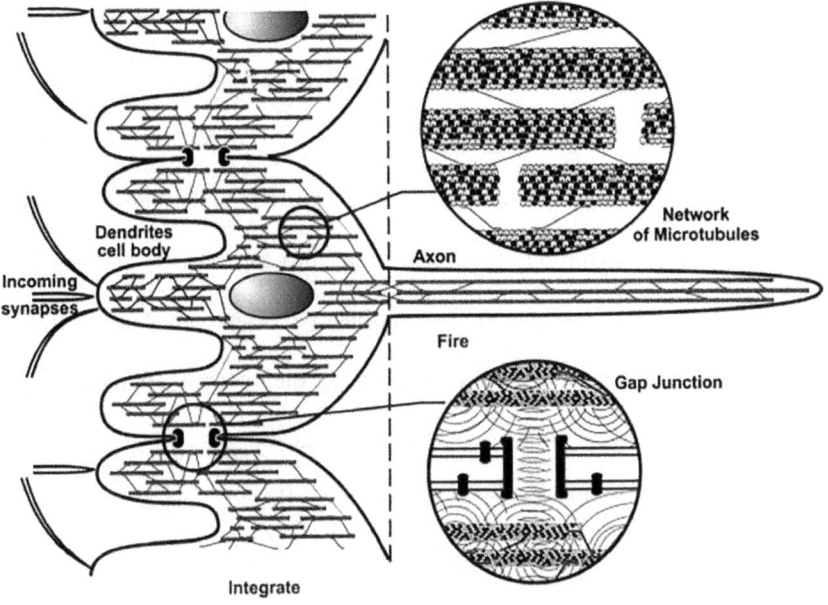

Figure 1: Dendritic-Somatic Integration and Microtubules[126]

---

[126] Hameroff and Penrose: "Consciousness in the Universe: A Review of Orch OR Theory" "In dendrites and cell body/soma involved in integration (left), microtubules are interrupted and of mixed polarity, interconnected by microtubule-associated proteins (MAPs) in recursive networks (upper circle, right). Dendritic–somatic integration (with contribution from microtubule processes) can trigger axonal firings to the next synapse. Microtubules in axons are unipolar and continuous. Gap junctions synchronize dendritic membranes, and may enable entanglement and collective integration among microtubules in adjacent neurons (lower circle right)"

reduction theory concerning microtubules which contain bits of quantum information at the subatomic level and are directly related to consciousness, as corroborated by other research[127]. My position on consciousness is a type of emergentism regarding consciousness being more than the sum of the parts of dark energy in microtubules. "As systems acquire increasingly higher degrees of organizational complexity, they begin to exhibit novel properties which in some sense transcend the properties of their constituent parts, and behave in ways that cannot be predicted on the basis of the laws governing simpler systems"[128]. It also regards the processes that take place which are explainable by quantum physics and not just materialism.

In Orch OR, as it is known in short, microtubule quantum computations take place during the integration of dendrites and soma cells, and the selected results regulate axonal firings to control behavior. Indeed, microtubule resonant vibrations have been compared to music, particularly anharmonic Indian Raga[129]. "Consciousness depends on anharmonic vibrations of

---

[127] Recent evidence demonstrated that anesthetics (which selectively erase consciousness) act on microtubules, rather than as was generally assumed, membrane receptors (Emerson et al, 2013).

[128] Jaegwon Kim, "Making Sense of Emergence"

[129] Ghosh et. al, Information 2014, 5: "Each resonant vibration has several harmonic and inharmonic overtones, heights of both columns are astronomical."

microtubules inside neurons, similar to certain kinds of Indian music, but unlike Western music which is harmonic," Hameroff explains. These anharmonic vibrations are the direct vibrations of dark energy.

Microtubules are the cell component that contain Leibniz's monad[130]. A monad is an indivisible substance or building block that inscribes space and time[131]. The information of these monads is basically imperishable even past the life of the microtubule cell[132] and the information survives when released from the microtubules at the quantum level. Each microtubule holds a lifeworld of consciousness. The difference between microtubules and monads is that there are an infinite number of monads at the root level, for Leibniz, while microtubules, which are a material entity, exist finitely. We could construct an ontology of consciousness out of the Leibnizian monad[133].

---

[130] Leibniz, Monadology, 1: "The monad, of which we shall speak here, is nothing but a simple substance that enters into composites; simple, that is, without parts."
[131] Leibniz, Monadology, §1: "The monad, about which we shall speak here, is nothing other than a simple substance which enters into compounds, 'simple' meaning 'without parts'."
[132] Leibniz, Monadology, §4 "No dissolution of these elements need be feared, and there is no conceivable way in which a simple substance can perish naturally".
[133] "So the Leibnizean commitment to ultimate simple substances or monads is perfectly consistent with the infinite divisibility of space after all – but (and here is Kant's characteristic twist) it can only be maintained by explicitly adopting the

Although they could be compared to souls, monads are basically building blocks of souls as substances, and are more basic[134]. In string theory, we can say that the vibrating strings are monads or microtubules.

Newtonian conception of forces acting at a distance (in this case a short-range repulsive force acting at a very small distance given by the radius of its "sphere of activity")." ix, Front Matter of Metaphysical Foundations of Natural Science

[134] Leibniz, *Monadology*, §19: "But as sensation is something more than a simple perception, I hold that the general name of 'monads' and 'entelechies' is sufficient for simple substances which only have perceptions, and that only those whose perception is more distinct and is accompanied by memory should be called souls."

II. Leibniz's Monadology and Quantum Physics

Gottfried Wilhelm Leibniz was heavily influenced and inspired by ancient Chinese philosophy and spirituality. He believed that it was the most accurate in describing the nature of the cosmos, more so than Western philosophy. The *I Ching* indirectly influenced his Monadology in that Leibniz noticed a similarity between the trigrams and his binary arithmetic. Leibniz was interested in binary systems in order to make an ontological statement. He wanted to use a system of 1's and 0's to show how God could build the universe from the features of unity and nothingness. A feature of a substance in Leibniz's ontological system is its genuine unity which can be likened to Brahman[135]. Leibniz's only source on China was his correspondence with Jesuit missionaries[136] who communicated with Confucian scholar officials. His correspondence was primarily with Joachim Bouvet, who portrayed the *I Ching*

---

[135] Letter to Arnaud, G II 76/AG 79: "A substantial unity requires a thoroughly indivisible and naturally indestructible being, since its notion includes everything that will happen to it, something which can be found neither in shape nor in motion (both of which involve something imaginary, as I could demonstrate), but which can be found in a soul or substantial form, on the model of what is called *me*."
[136] Perkins, Francis. Leibniz and China: *A Commerce of Light*, p. 28. The spirit of natural theology allowed for exchange between the cultures of China and Europe, both of which admired Confucian thought. The Jesuit missionaries primarily derived their knowledge of customs from Confucian literati scholars.

as a text of natural theology which pluralistically allowed for knowledge of God to be present in pagan texts. Bouvet saw the six lines of the I Ching hexagram as symbolic of the six days God took to make the heavens and the earth.

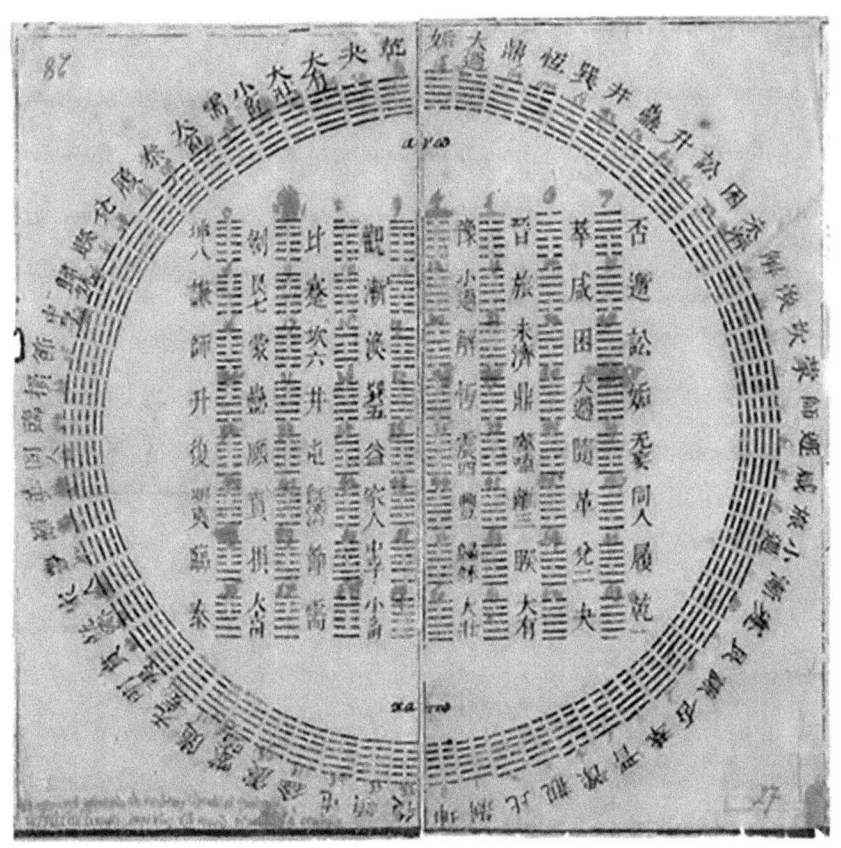

Figure 2: Leibniz's I Ching woodcut

Each of the six lines in an I Ching hexagram is a broken and changing yin line, or an unbroken, unchanging yang line. The yin represents what is transcendent[137], and the yang what is imminent. They are produced from a binary such as a coin or yarrow toss, and the sixty-four possible combinations of hexagrams represent all possible scenarios on Earth; all possible patterns of changes in the universe. Alongside changing or unchanging lines, the wave-particle duality of Niels Bohr can also be conceived of as a binary. An electron changes from a particle to a wave when its activity is not observed. Whether a hexagram contains changing lines can correspond to whether an electron particle changes to a wave at any point in a set of six experiments. Change or process happens unobserved, or unaffected causally by consciousness as energy.

---

[137] Deleuze and Guattari, *What is Philosophy*, Geophilosophy, p. 89: "Hexagrams are combinations of continuous and discontinuous features deriving from one another according to the levels of a spiral that figures the set of moments through which the transcendent descends."

The Image

Thunder comes resounding out of the earth:
The Image of Enthusiasm.
Thus the ancient kings made music
In order to honor merit,
And offered it with splendor
To the Supreme Deity,
Inviting their ancestors to be present.

Changing Lines

Changing yin at the bottom means:
Enthusiasm that expresses itself
Brings misfortune.

Changing yin in the second place means:
Firm as a rock. Not a whole day.
Perseverance brings good fortune.

Changing yin in the third place means:
Enthusiasm that looks upward creates remorse.
Hesitation brings remorse.

Changing yang in the fourth place means:
The source of enthusiasm.
He achieves great things.
Doubt not.
You gather friends around you
As a hair clasp gathers the hair.

Changing yin in the fifth place means:
Persistently ill, and still does not die.

Changing yin at the top means:
Deluded enthusiasm.
But if after completion one changes,
There is no blame.

Figure 3: An Example of an I Ching Reading

We might use Leibniz's theory of monads and the *I Ching* to describe how electrons change into waves only when not measured or observed. A particle might be said to be an immanent state of unity while a wave is a transcendent state of non-unity (dispersal) or nothingness. The yin on the *I Ching*, representing change, might signify the change to a wave in the quantum slit experiment or a change back to a particle. The change from a particle to a wave is probabilistic and part of a pattern of detectable changes, much like presence of yin or broken lines on the *I Ching*[138][139]. When scientists try to predict or detect which slit a photon passes through or display absolute and objective control or knowledge over the experiment, it does not change to a wave or display an interference pattern.

---

[138] Much like the quantum slit experiment, we can use the I Ching to demonstrate the role that consciousness plays upon matter. Robert Lanza, Biocentrism, p. 81: The "behavior of subatomic particles—indeed all particles and objects—is inextricably linked to the presence of an observer. Without the presence of a conscious observer, they at best exist in an undetermined state of probability waves. ... Without consciousness, "matter" dwells in an undetermined state of probability. Any universe that could have preceded consciousness only existed in a probability state". Arkady Plotnitsky, *Epistemology and Probability*, p. 212, also discusses probability and the wave function.

[139] Zabriskie, *Atom and Archetype*, p. xxxix

Perhaps the photon remains concentrated into a particle when observed because of the interference caused by measurement. This can be explained by the Heisenberg Uncertainty Principle, in which one can never know both the velocity and position of a photon particle at once[140]. This is why when the velocity of a photon particle through one or both slits becomes known scientists forgo knowing which slit it passed through (its position or location).

The double slit experiment is significant because it shows how measurement as a form of absolute control changes the form of light by causing it to appear as a photon or particle. Observation shuts down the wave function temporarily. That might indicate that in its natural unobserved state,

---

[140] Heisenberg, W., *Die Physik der Atomkerne*, Taylor & Francis, 1952, p. 30. "It can be expressed in its simplest form as follows: One can never know with perfect accuracy both of those two important factors which determine the movement of one of the smallest particles—its position and its velocity. It is impossible to determine accurately both the position and the direction and speed of a particle at the same instant." Elmira A. Isaeva, "Human Perception of Physical Experiments and the Simplex Interpretation of Quantum Physics," p. 47: "The problem of quantum physics, as a choice of one alternative at quantum measurement and a problem of philosophy as to how consciousness functions, is deeply connected with relations between these two. It is quite possible that in solving these two problems, it is likely that experiments in the quantum mechanics will include workings of a brain and consciousness, and it will then be possible to present a new basis for the theory of consciousness."

light is a wave[141]. An electron exists in oscillating wave form until measured, and measurement seems to fix the electron in particle form. Perhaps consciousness causes interference because it, too, corresponds to the wave function.

A. Pre-established harmony

Pre-established harmony, for Leibniz, can be affirmed as something that evidences God's existence. According to Leibniz's doctrine of pre-established harmony, 1) no state of a created substance is caused by some state of another created substance; 2) every non-initial, non-miraculous state of a created substance has as a real cause some previous state of that very substance; and 3) each created substance is programmed at creation such that all its natural states and actions are carried out in conformity with all the natural states and actions of every other created substance. There is pre-established harmony

---

[141] According to quantum physics, the watched pot may never actually boil.

between all substances in the universe[142]. This applies to the way that the soul influences the body[143].

This implies that all harmony is an intra-substantial coincidence rather than something that is inter-causally produced. For example, whether light appears as a particle photon or a wave does not depend on whether it previously appeared as a particle or wave, much as a hexagram on the *I Ching* is not caused by the previous hexagram reading, according to the doctrine of pre-established harmony.

We can compare Leibniz's pre-established harmony with that of Goethe. In Leibniz, harmony signifies that all parts are operating in conjunction with the existence of all other parts. Leibniz holds to a micro-harmony in

---

[142] Leibniz, *Monadology*, §78: "The soul follows its own laws, and the body likewise follows its own, and they coincide by virtue of the pre-established harmony between all substances, since they are all representations of one and the same universe"

[143] Leibniz, *Monadology*, §80: "Descartes recognised that souls cannot impart force to bodies because there is always the same quantity of force in matter. However, he believed that the soul could change the direction of bodies. But this is because the law of nature which also affirms the conservation of the same total direction in matter was not known in his day. If he had noticed this, he would have come across my system of pre-established harmony." Pre-established harmony alone constitutes the union of the soul and body, for Leibniz. We can consider this in substantial harmony as being a type of mind-body interactionism.

structure[144] as well as a harmony of events and multiverses[145]. Leibniz states that there is no chaos[146] in the universe. Harmony also happens on the macrocosmic level in Goethe, where the motions of the planets in orbit along with the existence of divine angelic beings produce a type of cosmic music in their harmony[147]; one that abides by mathematical structure. Goethe also

---

[144] Leibniz, *Monadology, §63:* " Every monad is in its way a mirror of the universe, and the universe is regulated in a perfect order, it must be the case that there is also an order in whatever represents it, that is, in the perceptions of the soul, and consequently in the body, in accordance with which the universe is represented in it." ... Leibniz, *Monadology, §56:* "Now this interconnection, or this accommodation of all created things to each other and of each to all the rest, means that each simple substance has relations which express all the others, and that consequently it is a perpetual living mirror of the universe"

[145] Leibniz, *Monadology, §54:* "And this reason can only be found in the fittingness, or in the degrees of perfection, which these worlds contain, each possible world having the right to claim existence in proportion to the perfection it contains. [Thus there is nothing which is wholly arbitrary"

[146] Leibniz, *Monadology,* §69: "Thus there is nothing uncultivated, nothing sterile, nothing dead in the universe, no chaos, no confusions, except in appearance."

[147] Goethe, *Faust* trans. Bayard Taylor, p. 20: "How each the whole its substance gives, Each in the other works and lives! Like heavenly forces rising and descending, their golden urns reciprocally lending, with wings that winnow blessing from Heaven through Earth I see them pressing, Filling the All with Harmony unceasing!"

alludes to multiverses[148]. However, we can criticize Goethe for believing there is divine harmony all throughout the universe. There wouldn't be a constant harmony produced, so much as sites of harmony sporadically punctuating sites of discord. For example, the entropy or chaos[149] of black holes or points in space where there is singularity in the breakdown of space and time, as well as times when a meteor is close to hitting Earth, would be examples of disharmony, and of events happening unpredictably and defying the harmonic order.

In quantum entanglement, we would have photons aligning at the same frequency and meeting in harmony. A wave state would render discordant, anharmonic structures in the process of achieving an overall harmony which is its end approximation. The wave and the sound of disharmony is naturally Otherly to the human senses, as dark energy is.

---

[148] Goethe, *Faust*, trans. Priest, p. 231: "For where in a pure orbit ruleth Nature/ All worlds unite and blend in harmony"

[149] Deleuze and Guattari, *What is Philosophy*, p. 118: "Chaos is defined not so much by its disorder as by the infinite speed with which every form taking shape in it vanishes. It is a void that is not a nothingness but a virtual, containing all possible particles and drawing out all possible forms, which spring up only to disappear immediately, without consistency or reference, without consequence. l Chaos is an infinite speed of birth and disappearance."

III. On Affirmation

Some physicists believe that there are virtually an infinite number of universes where alternate histories, that is, a series of events, are occurring. If the universe is constantly expanding, this is potentially true. According to string theory, the number of multiverses the human brain can distinguish is $10^{10^{16}}$, or 10 with 16 zeros. The mathematical laws that these alternate universes abide by would allow for unimaginable events to happen[150].

Leibniz believes, in his *Theodicy*, that Earth is where the best of all possible worlds is constantly occurring[151]. This is a version of Nietzsche's

---

[150] Max Tegmark, *Our Mathematical Universe,* p. 401, on higher-level multiverses: "There's a fourth level of parallel universes that's vastly larger than the three we've encountered so far, corresponding to different mathematical structures. ... Whereas all the parallel universes at Levels I, II and III obey the same fundamental mathematical equations (describing quantum mechanics, inflation, etc.), Level IV parallel universes dance to the tunes of different equations, corresponding to different mathematical structures."

[151] Leibniz, Monadology, §53: "Now as there is an infinity of possible universes in the ideas of God, and as only one of them can exist, there must be a sufficient reason for God's choice, determining him to one rather than to another."
Austin Farrer, *Theodicy,* p. 33: "God does not explore it, he simply possesses it all: the whole region of the possible is but a part of the content of his infinite mind. So among all possible creatures he chooses the best and creates it".

eternal return where every single event in this world and universe can be amor-fati ed or eternally affirmed[152]. It is because God has created all monads with an engrained set of histories to turn out for the better that there is affirmability by design[153]. Spinoza, too, believes that the world has been created by God with perfect reason.

Affirmation means seeing eternal harmony in this universe[154]. Harmony, including pre-established harmony, would involve faith that the universe's

---

Leibniz, *Theodicy,* p. 69: " God, having chosen the most perfect of all possible worlds, had been prompted by his wisdom to permit the evil which was bound up with it, but which still did not prevent this world from being, all things considered, the best that could be chosen." In the view of the contemporary physicists, Leibniz seems to hold that the universe is the mind of God.

[152] Nietzsche, *The Gay Science* trans. Walter Kaufmann, p. 273, §341: "This life as you now live it and have lived it, you will have to live once more and innumerable times more; and there will be nothing new in it, but every pain and every joy and every thought and sigh and everything unutterably small or great in your life will have to return to you, an in the same succession and sequence--even this spider and this moonlight between the trees, and even this moment and I myself. The eternal hourglass of existence is turned upside down again and again, and you with it, speck of dust!"

[153] Leibniz, *Theodicy,* p. 56: "Everything happens of necessity, through the concatenation of causes"

[154] Nietzsche, *The Gay Science* trans. Walster Kaufmann, p. 223, §276: "Amor fati: let that be my love henceforth! I do not want to wage war against what is ugly. I do not

components would be playing out their respective parts, both at the macro and micro levels, by design. This would apply to dark energy at its macro and micro scales. Leibniz's hierarchy of monads implies that the harmony of the macro-physical universe parallels the micro-physical. Just as there is harmony at the macro-physical level of planets in Goethe, there is supposed harmony at the micro-physical, of quantum particles, monads or microtubules. However, the harmony in the latter is really a type of anharmonic harmony, because microtubules and monads display quantum activity that is anharmonic in structure[155]. Affirmation would be of anharmonic structures playing out overall and eventual harmony. *Disharmony happens when processes like wave-states are viewed in isolation.* There are an infinite number of monads[156] in this harmonic-anharmonic structure at the micro level, for Leibniz[157].

---

want to accuse; I do not even want to accuse those who accuse. Looking away shall be my only negation. And all in all and on the whole: some day I wish to be only a Yes-sayer! "

[155] Arkady Plotnitsky, *Epistemology and Probability*, p. 212: "Von Neumann argues, in his ensemble framework, that if quantum mechanics is correct, the laws of nature at the ultimate level of its constitution would have to be noncausal."

[156] Leibniz, *Monadology*, §65: "Each portion of matter is not only divisible to infinity"

[157] Goethe, *Faust* trans. Priest, p. 33: Mephistopheles: "A man, the microcosmic fool, down in his soul / Is wont to think himself a whole, / But I'm part of the Part which at the first was all, / Part of the Darkness that gave birth to Light." Compared to the

We tend to think of heaven as being vastly infinite, in terms of a cosmic harmony. However, Leibniz's structure of monads is infinitesimal. This would bring new meaning to Leo Tolstoy's "The Kingdom of Heaven is within you." The microcosm would also be vastly infinite like the macrocosm, and allow for the soul to exist in an imperishable quantum state upon death by occupying virtually any realm or dimension in the multiverse[158]. I will later describe the multiverse theory in the theory of Quantum Immortality, in Chapter Ten.

---

deist Leibniz, Goethe does not believe that there is harmony at the level of the soul due to the existence of sin.

[158] Leibniz, *Monadology, §57*: "In the same way it happens that, because of the infinite multitude of simple substances, there are just as many different universes, which are nevertheless merely perspectives of a single universe according to the different points of view of each monad."

IV. The Archetypal Psyche

Psychology pioneer Carl Jung wrote extensive letters to the physicist Wolfgang Pauli[159]. Both arrived to the conclusion that the nature of the psyche can be likened to that of the atomic archetype[160]. Like the atom as a fundamental particle unit of matter, the soul or psyche can be considered archetypal in form and structure, in terms of the way that it can then change

---

[159] *Atom and Archetype: The Pauli/Jung Letters, 1932-1958.*

[160] *Atom and Archetype,* p. xvii: An archetype is "an intrinsically abstract predetermined formal factor of the psychic life; to a certain extent, the psychic representatives of the instincts, which is why, at all times and in all places, the archetypes manifest themselves in identical fashion in so-called archetypal images (d. religious symbols) or archetypal patterns of behavior." Carl Jung in *The Interpretation of Nature and the Psyche,* quoted in *Atom and Archetype,* p. xxix: "As the phenomenal world is an aggregate of the processes of atomic magnitude, it is naturally of the greatest importance to find out whether, and if so how, the photons (shall we say) enable us to gain a definite knowledge of the reality underlying the mediative energy processes ... Light and matter both behave like separate particles and also like waves. This ... obliged us to abandon, on the plane of atomic magnitudes, a causal description of nature in the ordinary space-time system, and in ill place to set up invisible fields of probability in multidimensional spaces." It is interesting that Jung and not Pauli has written this, as a result of the two's correspondence and exchange of terms.

according to a set pattern[161]. We might compare the way Leibniz has likened the soul to a monad[162]: It is multiplicitous and generic, as well as polymorphous in its potentiality of forms[163]. Any person can become neurotic or psychotic when exposed to certain environmental factors which are nowadays laid out in the Diagnostic Statistical Manual. Hence, the archetype is a perfect way to illustrate the structure of the subjective psyche and its possible

---

[161] *Atom and Archetype*, p. xxxii: "For Jung, archetypes are not structures but "habitual currents of psychic energy," "systems of readiness for action." Pauli refers to them as "statistical laws with primary probabilities.· These exist before and beyond the only personal data of the individual time-and-space-bound ego and so further relativize it."

[162] Leibniz, *Monadology*, 19: "If we wish to give the name 'soul' to everything that has perceptions and appetites in the general sense I have just explained, then all simple substances or created monads could be called souls; but as sensation is something more than simple perception, I believe the general name 'monad' or 'entelechy' suffices for simple substances that have perception only, and that the name "soul" should be given only to those in which perception is more distinct and accompanied by memory. "

[163] Leibniz, *Monadology,* 16: "We ourselves experience a multitude in a simple substance, when we find that the least thought of which we are aware involves a variety in its object. Thus all those who admit that the soul is a simple substance should admit this multitude in the monad"

metamorphoses[164]; we could also examine genetic factors affecting a healthy person's brain. In addition, I liken the soul to an atom or archetype because the change of a particle to a wave, like the changes that occur to a psyche, are dependent on whether an observer is present; the presence of outside consciousness or energies.

Our energy or electrons can be entangled with that of others from far away. People can exchange energy with those hundreds of miles away[165]. The

---

[164] Beverley Zabriskie, *Atom and Archetype,* p. Xxxii: "Jung's notion of the archetypes of the collective unconscious implied, so to speak, a supercharge, an "overplus," of energy emerging from those "fields· of interrelated experience that the human psyche is predisposed to find significant. For Jung, archetypes are not structures but "habitual currents of psychic energy," "systems of readiness for action." Pauli refers to them as "statistical laws with primary probabilities"

[165] Alfred Whitehead in *Modes of Thought,* pg. 188: "Matter has been identified with energy, and energy is sheer activity; the passive substratum composed of self-identical enduring bits of matter has been abandoned, so far as concerns any fundamental description. ... The modern point of view is expressed in terms of energy, activity, and the vibratory differentiations of space-time. Any local agitation shakes the whole universe. The distant effects are minute, but they are there. The concept of matter presupposed simple location. Each bit of matter was self-contained, localized in a region with a passive, static network of spatial relations, entwined in a uniform relational system from infinity to infinity and from eternity to eternity. But in the modern concept the group of agitations which we term matter is fused into its environment."

energy state of consciousness/ the soul means that Spirit is collective, as Hegel and others described (see Section 3)[166].

---

[166] Hegel, The Phenomenology of Spirit, §488: "The spirit of this world is spiritual essence permeated by a self-consciousness which knows itself to be directly present as a self-existent particular, and knows that essence as an objective actuality over itself."

Chapter Four. The Multiverse

I. With and Against Goethe

We previously applied the First Thermodynamic law concerning energy to the scientific phenomenon of consciousness, stating that consciousness as energy can neither be created nor destroyed. It must only change form between higher and lower order states at all stages of its physical composition. That means that all we are essentially looking at in the universe are changes of energy (not matter, as the materialist claims!). We can take into the concentration of energy and the frequency of such energy, along with the types of matter or condensed energy in its composition[167]. If the essence of a thing metaphysically is dependent specifically on the configuration of space-time and frequency of quantum vibrations as well as condensation of energy into substances, then it is like music; we can take all these factors into consideration when we say it is like the harmony of Goethe's spheres[168].

---

[167] Alfred Whitehead In *Modes of Thought*, pg. 188, describes the "vibratory differentiations of space-time"

[168] Goethe, *Faust* trans. George Madison Priest, Prologue: pg. 7: Raphael: "The Sun intones, in ancient journey with brother-spheres, a rival song, fulfilling its predestined journey"

In a harmonic view of the universe, such as in Goethe, all planetary and microcosmic (quantum) activity corresponds to harmonic patterns. While we might attribute this behavior to the wave function, we can say that there is individual disharmony at the quantum level with the inconsistent form that photons take on. They abide by an anharmonic law, however[169]. Waves stop acting as waves and become particles when observed. If the wave function is harmonic, we can describe the act of perturbations in the wave function as anharmonic. Photons act like photons only when observed. Whether this corresponds to a rhythm overall is uncertain. It is only at times that there is activity at the micro level of the universe that proceeds as if orchestrated. So, too, can we say for the macro level, at the level of substance composition of macro entities such as stars and galaxies which go out of being in conditions of singularity and display disharmony and lack of physical regularity of matter, time and space. At the micro level it is partially disharmonic, as it is at the macro level.

---

[169] Arkady Plotnitsky, *Chaosmologies,* p. 45: "[Quantum mechanics] is fundamentally statistical: it involves chance irreducible to any underlying causality. It is not 46 Paragraph only that the state of the system at a given point gives us no help in predicting its behaviour or allows us to assume it to be causally determined, if unpredictable, at later points, although that such is the case experimentally is important."

At the macro level, that of the universe, there is entropy because space and time are not constants and only relative. Space is constantly inflating or expanding, except at certain points such as the solar system. This would mean that Goethe's harmony of spheres only applies to certain points of space in the universe that do not appear as a black hole from outside[170].

---

[170] Max Tegmark, *Our Mathematical Universe*, p. 147

II. Deleuzian Multiplicity

It would be wrong to characterize a photon as a multiplicity. There is change involved as far as a photon particle changes to wave form and back again, but to describe it as being in constant flux, which is a feature of a multiplicity[171], is to characterize its sporadic changes too broadly. However, we might say that consciousness is a multiplicity insofar as it is dark energy, or electrons constantly being entangled. Because matter and mind are both composed of electrons being entangled, there is no limit to the entanglement that is occurring; consciousness is in perpetual entanglement with the objects and other consciousnesses in its environment.

---

[171] Deleuze's examples of multiplicity are race, class, gender, language, state, society, person, and party. All these are socially constructed categories, unlike consciousness or a photon/wave.

III. Embracing Quantum Paradox

The wave-particle duality or complementarity can be conceived of as a paradox. Ontologically, the photon has no one form. This is counterintuitive. Matter at its fundamental level is both wave and particle in nature, but the form they take on changes. In Brahman, the level of ultimate or absolute truth is beyond observation. The conclusion we can derive from the quantum slit experiment differs, as there are more than a couple interpretations[172].

---

[172] Michael Epperson, *Quantum Physics and the Philosophy of Alfred North Whitehead*, ix: Quantum mechanics seems to entail two competing and incompatible fundamental descriptions of nature, and this leaves one with three alternatives: (i) to characterize nature as fundamentally particulate wherein wave-like properties are an abstraction; (ii) to characterize nature as fundamentally wave-like wherein particulate properties are an abstraction; (iii) to pass through these two horns and deny that nature is capable of fundamental characterization at all (apart from this sanction itself, of course) such that we merely characterize our complementary *experiences* of nature as wave-like or particle-like depending on the circumstances, rather than characterizing nature herself. To each of these viewpoints we can associate various theorists--Einstein, for example, to the first, Schrödinger to the second, Bohr to the third, and so forth"

Chapter Five. The Physicists' Heaven

I. Dimensions

I will be describing the types of matter in the universe, as well as alternate and parallel universes in the chapter. According to contemporary theorists, there exist an infinite number of universes, or multiverses, in which the ideal happens. According to Leibniz, what is happening in this particular world is said to be the best possible situation that can happen given the constraints of space and time applying to the world. In all parallel universes it is believed that there are worse things and events happening.

We might also attribute this feature of eternity to the Universe,[173] where the universe is continually repeating its sequences of events and in reenacting scenarios. Gradually the universe unentangles itself and approaches resolution. Eventually, in this universe one approaches the ideal scenario that can be affirmed in itself as the resolution of events, where the ideal is the actual. There needs to be no parallel universe where something better is happening.

---

[173] Robert Lanza, Biocentrism, p. 163: "A Big Bang means the universe was born, and that therefore it must someday die, even if no one knows whether this is just one of an endlessly repeating temporal cycle of Bangs, or even if other universes exist concurrently. Thus, eternity cannot be disproved"

The contemporary physicists believe in eleven different dimensions; so what's not to say that beyond space and time in the first four, the seven different layers of heaven in the monotheistic religions[174] is contained in the next seven?

Superstring Theory posits that the universe exists in ten different dimensions. Beyond the three standard dimensions, the fourth dimension is

---

[174] In the three Abrahamic religious belief systems/traditions, or monotheistic religious traditions (which first began in ancient Mesopotamia, and is seen in Judaeo-Christianity and Kabbalah, as well as Islam), there are Seven Layers of Heaven, each corresponding to states of the Spirit/Soul, and are also loosely seen in Hinduism, Jainism, and Buddhism, as well as, to an extent, Zoroastrianism. The 7th Heaven (Araboth): This is where God or the Lord resides. It is made of divine light, and it is where he resides with his angels of dread, fear, and grace (the Ophanim [Wheels] and Seraphim) VII. Araboth (ערבות) = deserts. 6th Heaven (Makhon): This is where Moses resides. It is constructed of garnets and rubies. VI. Machon (מכון) = city, established place. 5th Heaven (Ma'on): Visited by the prophet Zephaniah, it is where Abraham, the knight of faith, lives with the Avenging Angel, Gilead? Abaddon (Apollyon)?. This is the Universe's Courthouse. V. Ma'on (מעון) = refuge.4th Heaven (Zebhul): Of white gold, it is where Enoch and the Angel of Tears, Cassiel. IV. Zebul (זבול) = habitation.3rd Heaven (Shehaqim): It is here that Joseph resides, in a place made of pearls and other dazzling gems. III. Shehaqim (שחקים) = clouds.2nd Heaven: Of gold, it is where Jesus Christ and John the Baptist reside. II. Raki'a (רקיע) = Expanse, canopy:1st Heaven (Vilon): It is where Adam and Eve reside, with the angels of each star. The first layer of heaven is composed of silver. I. Vilon (וילון) = Veil, curtain.

time[175]. The fifth and sixth dimensions are where the notion of possible worlds arises. The seventh dimension continues the notion of possible worlds, and the eighth dimension details possible histories that branch out infinitely. In the ninth dimension, we can compare all of these histories, and in the tenth dimension we find that all that is imaginable and possible has been covered. This is where we arrive at the number of multiverses, ten with sixteen zeroes.

There are regions in the multiverse which are impossible to reach by space shuttle, even if one were to travel infinitely. It is these dimensions which I suggest one travels to in death, when one's consciousness is freed from microtubules in the brain[176]. If space is not a constant, it is in dimensions not confined by the typical definition of space that the soul as quantum information can inhabit and visit, while a space shuttle cannot. The view of multiple worlds or universes plays a role in the theory of Quantum

---

[175]Robert Lanza, *Biocentrism,* p. 97: "Time appears to be indispensable in just one area— thermodynamics, whose second law has no meaning at all without the passage of time. Thermodynamics' second law describes entropy (the process of going from greater to lesser structure, like the bottom of your clothes closet). Without time, entropy cannot happen or even make sense."

[176] See Chapter 9, on the Bardo Theol, and Chapter 10, on Eben Alexander's *Proof of Heaven*

Immortality and the Many Minds Approach, which have been discussed by the physicists Max Tegmark, Michael Lockwood, and Hans Moravec, among others. In Quantum Immortality, consciousness stays alive even though the conscious being dies; this is a view that will be explored further in Chapter Ten. In other words, the being never really dies. When confronted with death, the mind will always transport itself to alternate realities where it survives otherwise fatal events. These realities take place in parallel universes or alternate dimensions whose infinity[177] is based upon the infinitely expanding space of the universe we have addressed in Chapter One. Tegmark states that "If the Many Worlds idea is correct, the experimenter will discover that she is immortal[178]."

---

[177] Michael Lockwood, *Mind, Brain, and the Quantum:* "Consciousness is tied to one amongst a potential infinity of what, in the context of quantum mechanics, are known as representations"

[178] Marcus Chown, "Dying to Know" in *New Scientist,* December 1997

II. Brahman and Collective Consciousness

If the Self or Consciousness upon death becomes Universal substance (Brahman), it seems that there would be no more individuation, as in atman. Then we can question if there is any more multiplicity, and whether Universal substance means that all is homogenous. It would be true that in its parallel dimension, Brahman is quantum entangled with itself. But this does not mean that it cannot also go through further changes. We cannot rule out If All becomes One, we can still differentiate individual consciousnesses in the All[179].

---

[179] See Chapter 9 and 10 on near death experiences and out-of-body experiences. Hegel, *Aesthetics*, p. 335: "But the Indian way of unifying the human self with Brahma is nothing but the steadily enhanced 'screwing oneself up' to this extreme abstraction itself, wherein not only the entire concrete content but even self-consciousness must perish before man can attain to this abstraction. Therefore the Indian knows no reconciliation and identity with Brahma in the sense of the human spirit's reaching knowledge of this unity; on the contrary, the unity consists for the Indian precisely in the fact that consciousness and self-consciousness and therefore all the content of the world and the inner worth of the man's own personality totally disappear."

III. Types of Matter

Interestingly enough, dark matter, the stuff that holds galaxies together, accounts for the majority of the Milky Way Galaxy[180]. Just four percent of the observable universe consists of known material such as atoms and subatomic particles. Scientists found out that half of all missing matter is in the dark matter that forms the gaps between galaxies as its gravitational glue, as well as in very dense baryon gases. Besides solid, liquid, gas, and plasma, there are degenerate states of matter, referring to matter at extremely high pressure in exotic states where matter is not baryonic[181]. They are supported by the Pauli exclusion principle, which prevents two fermionic particles from occupying the same quantum state.

---

[180] Sci-Tech Universe, Usman Abrar, October 2017

[181] Matter is not made of baryons or subatomic particles such as protons and neutrons

IV. Spacetime

In the fractal holographic cosmology, the building block of matter is a bit of information. It includes the quantum information that constitutes the soul upon death, when it is released from a quantum state in microtubules to one that preserves its content. Much like the fractal structure of consciousness, the space-time manifold is also recursive and fractal at infinite and infinitesimal levels. It was previously mentioned in Chapter I, Section I that spacetime is relative to consciousness. We may approach the phenomenon of consciousness as dark energy's process of inscription and manifestation of information in space-time, sometimes interacting with ordinary matter.

We as consciousness or conscious beings are not separate from this system; consciousness is inherent to it[182]. Space-time coordinates are embedded within our own being, the fabric of dark energy in space-time. A human entity and atom are both units with the function of processing information, albeit at very different relative scales of dimension, each with

---

[182] Robert Lanza, *Biocentrism,* 93: "The universe is simply the complete spatio-temporal logic of the self".

levels of quantum activity[183]. In the vitalist sense of Henri Bergson's *élan vital*, a being can be described as conscious, while an atom isn't. In the end, the information dynamics involved in the processes of consciousness and the dynamics involved in engendering the defining characteristics of space, time, energy and matter are one and the same in a symphony that is both harmonic and anharmonic. As we bridge physics with metaphysics we may surmise that consciousness does not only arise from the information dynamics of spacetime, but as dark energy is actually fundamental to the ordering and dynamics of reality itself in some ways.

The encoding capacity of a microtubule or monad, the material structure of *atmic* consciousness, is great[184]. As Leibniz stated, "As every present state of a simple substance is naturally a consequence of its preceding state, so its present is pregnant with its future"[185]. As it is at the quantum level, the reverberations consciousness carries throughout spacetime are very great. Space is said to be fractal and time is also fractally recursive. The life of a biological being represents a path of recursive feedback operations throughout the spatiotemporal dimension, progressing from a unique

---

[183] We can liken this view of panenpsychism to the ubiquity of Leibnizian monads which are psychophysical particles.

[184] Spinoza, *Ethics*, p. 5: "Every substance must be infinite."
[185] Leibniz, *Monadology*, 22.

encoded set of directions in the form of space-time coordinates onto a holographic spacememory field that is morphogenetic and maintains coherency in the vastly unified spatiotemporal network.

Chapter Six. The Void as Necessary for Creation

I. Black Holes and Dark Matter

In this chapter, the nature of the void and its relation to being, particularly the contrast of dark matter to the material discussed in the previous chapter, will be talked about. Dark matter, which is matter whose presence can only be discerned through its interactions with baryonic or ordinary matter and with gravity, composes most of the material universe, that is, 27% of its mass. Dark matter is considered the scaffolding of the universe and forms primordial black holes, black holes that were created in the first second of the universe's existence. 68-73% of the universe is dark energy, a primordial form of this dark matter that repels gravity. It has been mentioned that it contributes to the expansion of the universe--the creation of more space, and that a variant of dark energy composes consciousness.

It is notable that dark matter has never directly been observed, compared to the observable universe, which forms just four percent of the universe and consists of baryonic material, atoms and subatomic particles. Dark matter has continued to elude detection since it was first theorized, instead making its presence known only through its gravitational effects on objects in space. Due to black holes being composed of dark matter, "the surface gravity is the same everywhere on the event horizon of a time-independent black hole[186]."

A black hole is a void-like entity in which the escape velocity, the speed one must reach to escape some massive body, is greater than the speed of light[187]. Electron-degenerate matter is found inside white dwarf stars. Electrons remain bound to atoms but are able to transfer to adjacent atoms. Neutron-degenerate matter is found in neutron stars. Vast gravitational pressure compresses atoms so strongly that the electrons are forced to combine with protons via inverse beta-decay, resulting in a superdense conglomeration of neutrons. Normally free neutrons outside an atomic nucleus will decay with a half life of just under fifteen minutes, but in a neutron star, the decay is overtaken by inverse decay. Cold degenerate matter is also present in planets such as Jupiter and in the even more massive brown dwarfs, which are expected to have a core with metallic hydrogen. Because of the degeneracy, more massive brown dwarfs are not significantly larger. The black holes distort the distribution of mass in the early universe, adding a small fluctuation that has consequences hundreds of millions of years later, when the first stars begin to form.

---

[186] Hawking and Penrose, *The Nature of Space and Time*, p. 24
[187] Roger Penrose, *The Emperor's New Mind*, p. 332

Dark matter is unaffected by high temperatures because whatever its nature, it primarily interacts through gravity. Aggregating by mutual attraction, dark matter first collapsed into clumps called minihaloes, which provided a gravitational seed enabling normal matter to accumulate. Hot gas collapsed toward the mini-haloes, resulting in pockets of gas dense enough to further collapse on their own into the first stars.

A newly identified class of galaxies called red geysers harbor supermassive black holes with winds that produce a mysterious kind of "galactic warming" that, over the last few billion years, has turned huge numbers of galaxies into deserts devoid of fresh young stars. Astronomers had long wondered why certain galaxies did not demonstrate the creation of new stars, and had long suspected that the reason has something to do with the supermassive black hole that is at the centers of many galaxies. However, it turned out that it was actually the temperature of these galaxies that was the culprit. This means that dark matter, matter which cannot be seen, is responsible for the presence of stars.

II. The Meaning of Singularity

The universe emerged in a set of conditions where there was no time or space[188], matter or energy[189], or gravity[190]. Matter remained infinitely

---

[188] Stephen Hawking and Roger Penrose, *The Nature of Space and Time*, p. 20: "Because the singular points have to be cut out of the spacetime manifold, one cannot define the field equations there and one cannot predict what will come out of a singularity. With the singularity in the past the only way to deal with this problem seems to be to appeal to quantum gravity."

[189] Robert Lanza, Biocentrism, p. 5, "When a sixth grader asks the most basic question about the universe, such as, "What happened before the Big Bang?" The teacher, if knowledgeable enough, has an answer at the ready: "There was no time before the Big Bang, because time can only arise alongside matter and energy, so the question has no meaning. It's like asking what is north of the North Pole." Stephen Hawking and Roger Penrose, *The Nature of Space and Time*, p. 89, "The trouble with the hot big bang model is the trouble with all cosmology that has no theory of initial conditions: it has no predictive power. Because general relativity would break down at a singularity, anything could come out of a big bang."

[190] Roger Penrose, *The Emperor's New Mind*, p. 336: "Spacetime singularities are inevitable in situations of gravitational collapse." Such singularities refer to situations absent of space and time.

condensed, as in a black hole[191]. We can liken void space to creation[192] in the sense of the radical uncertainty and unpredictability of these conditions, including that of entropy[193]. Void spaces such as black holes demonstrate that the universe is ordered in harmony except for sites where there are perturbations in the harmonic function and matter is being reconfigured. In void spaces, we would have both undoing and annihilation of the material

---

[191] Stephen Hawking and Roger Penrose, *The Nature of Space and Time*, p. 20: "But the singularities that are predicted in the future seem to have a property that Penrose has called *cosmic censorship*. That is, they conveniently occur in places like black holes that are hidden from external observers.'

[192] Hawking and Penrose, *The Nature of Space and Time*, p. 27: Singularities occur in the big bang, in black holes, and in the big crunch (which might be regarded as a union of black holes. They also might appear as naked singularities. Related to this question is what is called *cosmic censorship*, namely the hypothesis that these naked singularities do not occur."

[193] Hawking and Penrose, *The Nature of Space and Time*, p. 26: "So it seems that black holes really do have intrinsic gravitational entropy. ... The intrinsic entropy means that gravity introduces an extra layer of unpredictability over and above the uncertainty usually associated with quantum theory. So Einstein was wrong when he said, "God does not play dice." Consideration of black holes suggests, not only that God does play dice, but that he sometimes confuses us by throwing them where they can't be seen."

before creation would begin anew[194].

We can equate the beginning of the universe to singularities or voids, where it is necessary that they remain cold for there to be the birth of new stars and galaxies. Anyone who has seen Hubble footage of matter spewing out of black holes knows the counterintuitive fact that it takes void to engender matter.

---

[194] Hawking and Penrose, *The Nature of Space and Time,* p. 59: "If information is lost in macroscopic black holes it should also be lost in processes in which macroscopic, virtual black holes appear because of quantum fluctuations of the metric."

III. Multiplicity and the Psyche

Much like it takes a set of void conditions to produce matter, it takes a set of limits in radical solitude to produce or create art or writing. This solitude was found in those such as Maurice Blanchot, Walter Benjamin or Marcel Proust, who fought insistently to defend their solitude and considered it a natural mode of existence[195]. However, Maurice Blanchot, as we will see, goes further with the neuter.

It was mentioned in Chapter One that the self, or consciousness is dispersed to different degrees toward a collectivity. The theme of multiplicity has previously been mentioned with regard to the self. Not only is the self a bundle of energies that is quantum entangled across space, but archepally it takes upon a multiplicity of forms. Upon death, both the soul and body change form; the soul is quantum information that separates from matter. Both are dissipated into the universe, dispersed across space as well as time.

Blanchot has utilized a number of techniques to introduce multiplicity

---

[195]Maurice Blanchot, *Thomas the Obscure*, p.16: "He was locked in combat with something inaccessible, foreign, something of which he could say: That doesn't exist, and which nevertheless filled him with terror as he sensed it wandering about in the region of his solitude. Having stayed up all night and all day with this being, as he tried to rest he was suddenly made aware that a second had replaced the first"

into his writing. These are fragmentary writing, dialogue, multiple typefaces, and the neuter (*le "il"*). Fragmentary writing can be seen in works such as *L'Attente l'Oubli* (*Awaiting Oblivion*) (1962), *La Pas au-delà* (*The Step Not Beyond*) (1973), and *L'Écriture du désastre* (*The Writing of the Disaster*) (1980). The defining essence of Blanchot's neuter is in the way that it critiques the notion of presence and ultimately displaces the subject who writes, which also displaces the idea of the subject as a locus of self-presencing[196].

"Beginning from the neuter, Blanchot displaces first the subject, then identity in general, and finally the present itself. The neuter ...taking the place of the subject in writing, detaches it from any relation to unity, displacing this relation in substituting for the I, always attached to a place, the he/it which is without place. The he/it can never be a speaking subject, can never have the presence of an I. The neuter displaces the subject as a rule of identity by introducing rupture into the idea of the self as presence and self-presence. If the he/it can substitute for any I, then the I is not full, living presence, but only a canonic abbreviation for a rule of identity."

---

[196] Insofar as Blanchot focuses on multiplicity, it seems he is focused on the idea of the self at death that is similar to Brahman.

The "I" as a rule of identity matches Jung's notion of the self as a generic archetype. The neuter replaces any singular notion of the I. We might equate this notion to Brahman. The neuter might place itself in dialectical opposition to the One, thus including itself conveniently in the whole. The neuter maintains identity unless, "... he/it, specified as the indeterminate term in order that the self in turn might determine itself as the major determinant, the never-subjected subject, is the very relation of the self to the other, in this sense: infinite or discontinuous, in this sense: relation always in displacement and in displacement in regard to itself, displacement also of that which would be without place"[197].

In Blanchot, we can thus see a collectivity of not-I in the self. We can utilize the neuter in Blanchot as an important cosmophenomenological metaphor[198]. Carolyn Bailey Gill states "that for Blanchot, writing establishes a relation with alterity that would appear to be strictly impersonal: a relation

---

[197] Maurice Blanchot, *The Step Not Beyond*, p. 5
[198] The tzimtzum/tsimtsum (Hebrew צמצום, meaning "contraction/ constriction/ condensation") is a Kabbalah Judaic term denoting Isaac Luria's doctrine that God started creation by "contracting" his Ein Sof (infinite) light to allow for a conceptual "vacant space" (ḥālāl happānuy, חלל הפנוי) into which new creative light could beam so that finite and seemingly independent realms could exist and energy be configured into matter. Much as Blanchot views the neuter as a stasis or an intermediary stage, J. Alfred Prufrock in T.S. Eliot's "Lovesong of J. Alfred Prufrock" says, "To have squeezed the universe into a ball/To roll it towards some overwhelming question,/To say: "I am Lazarus, come from the dead"

with the exteriority of *le neutre*"[199]. This exteriority is all the more counterintuitive because it occurs in a state of interiority and inwardness. We can see an example of the neuter making way for alterity in *Thomas the Obscure:*

"It was night itself. Images which constituted its darkness inundated him. He saw nothing, and, far from being distressed, he made this absence of vision the culmination of his sight. Useless for seeing, his eye took on extraordinary proportions, developed beyond measure, and, stretching out on the horizon, let the night penetrate its center in order to receive the day from it. And so, through this void, it was sight and the object of sight which mingled together. Not only did this eye which saw nothing apprehend something, it apprehended the cause of its vision. It saw as an object that which prevented it from seeing. Its own glance entered into it as an image, just when this glance seemed the death of all image"[200].

We can also regard the will to annihilation or non-ego in the neuter as important for self-development or self-actualization, much as a seeming annihilation must occur for there to be an alterity or reconstitution of elements

---

[199] Carolyn Bailey Gill, *Maurice Blanchot: The Demand of Writing*, p. 111

[200] Blanchot, *Thomas the Obscure*, p. 8

or matter in a black hole[201]. Dark energy is notable because due to its effect of repelling gravity, it is the only substance in the universe that can survive a black hole.

For Blanchot, as well as with Levinas and Derrida, however, there is an impossibility of death[202] where the narrators in his works repeatedly fail to reach a termination or end that death signifies. This is called the limit-experience, where awareness is irreducible and consciousness impersonal and anonymous *(le il y a)*. I will discuss the limit-experience again in Chapter IX.

---

[201] Jon Mills, *The Unconscious Abyss,* p. 73: "The death drive is a stimulus to anxiety whereas anxiety is understood as central to the ego's formation. Without the death drive, there would be no ego."

[202] Maurice Blanchot, "Literature and the Right to Death": "My impending death horrifies me because I see it as it is: no longer death, but the impossibility of dying."

Chapter Seven. Collective Consciousness Throughout History

I. Hegel and Eastern Thought

It has therefore been discussed how Brahman is a universal substance and represents the collective of consciousness. I will discuss collective consciousness in various thinkers. Georg W.F. Hegel's thought shows similarities to Vedanta Hinduism, especially regarding Spirit and self[203]. However, Hegel was wary of how Indian cult religion was a detriment toward human freedom[204]. Hegel equates Atman and Brahman[205]. Collective spirit is

---

[203] Peter C. Hodgson, *Hegel and Christian Theology*, p. 219: "Hegel's definition of the concept of religion--the unity, difference and reintegration of selfhood or spirit--is close to the core insight of Hinduism and Buddhism. Expressed in Hindu terms, spirit is *advaitic*, not-two, but also not simply one. Spiritual substance is one mediated by many through a spiralling process."

[204] Peter C. Hodgson, *Hegel and Christian Theology*, p. 223: "Universal substance, Brahman, with whom individual selves are in some sense identical, is not itself personal nor is it worshipped. By contrast with the God of Judaism, Brahman is the neuter one (*das Eine*), not the personal one (*der Eine*).

[205] T.M. Knox, *Aesthetics*, p. x: " God, the infinite spirit, is spirit only because he particularizes or embodies himself in a man (the Incarnation)." Hegel is described as a peculiar Christian.

tied to history (i.e. Zeitgeist) in various thinkers, including Hegel[206], Whitehead[207], and Benjamin[208].

Hegel described the consciousness of the era and mankind changing throughout history, as the self-awareness of man in history increases. In a way he was a process theologian like Alfred North Whitehead and Charles Hartshorne.

---

[206] Blanchot, *The Step Not Beyond*, p. 22: "Hegel (if his name invites us to think presence as all and the all as presence)"

[207] Whitehead, *Process and Reality*, p. 35: "The extensive continuity of the physical universe has usually been construed to mean that there is a continuity of becoming. But if we admit that 'something becomes,' it is easy, by employing Zeno's method, to prove that there can be no continuity of becoming. There is a becoming of continuity, but no continuity of becoming. The actual occasions are the creatures which become, and they constitute a continuously extensive world. In other words, extensiveness becomes, but 'becoming' is not itself extensive."

[208] Benjamin, Arcades Project, p. 365: "The degree of auratic saturation of human perception has fluctuated widely in the course of history. (In the Baroque, one might say, the conflict between cult value and exhibition value was variously played out within the confines of sacred art itself.) While these fluctuations await further clarification, the supposition arises that epochs which tend toward allegorical expression will have experienced a crisis of the aura [J77a,8]

II. Transcendentalism

The Over-soul in the 19th century Transcendentalists displays the influence of Vedanta Hinduism upon New England thinkers. In his essay "The Over-Soul," Ralph Waldo Emerson portrays the over-soul as the collective soul or Brahman, referring to it as "that Unity, that Over-soul, within which every man's particular being is contained and made one with all other[209]". In Brahman,

> "Meantime within man is the soul of the whole; the wise silence; the universal beauty, to which every part and particle is equally related; the eternal One. And this deep power in which we exist, and whose beatitude is all accessible to us, is not only self-sufficing and perfect in every hour, but the act of seeing and the thing seen, the seer and the spectacle, the subject and the object, are one."

Ralph Waldo Emerson refers to people as particles, with a physics metaphor similarly to the way that Leibniz has likened soul components to monads, or Spinoza to substances, or Jung to atoms. He also remarks that the whole is above observation, such as in the quantum slit experiment, and true to Indian Brahman. However, Emerson had read Emanuel Swedenborg, and mysticizes

---

[209] Ralph Waldo Emerson, "The Over-Soul," 1841

Brahman quite unlike the way that Hegel had wished Brahman to be portrayed.

III. Walter Benjamin and Jetztzeit

Walter Benjamin also described the soul as collective, in terms of its changes as a whole, and the self-consciousness of collective humanity increases or becomes more saturated throughout history in *Erfahrung* and *Jetztzeit* (the spontaneous now-moment of experiencing) as opposed to *Erleben* (passive and inauthentic experience). The increase is tied to the absence of human labor as well as an awareness of how the media is diminishing human experience. Erfahrung toward Jetztzeit is an increase in Schopenhauerian will and is tied to the ability of humankind to experience more genuinely, i.e. to be more self-aware and spiritually awake or conscious, and participate directly in their interactions with events and the external world in history.

We can directly contrast *Jetztzeit* from Hegel's authentic life in that it is entirely active and not mediated by rational pre-reflection. Collective's spirit's ability to experience authentically in history is not dependent in its degree of self-awareness. It's experience that is active and not passive. So it's entirely free from pre-reflection or rational thought, unlike in Hegel.

Chapter Eight. Atman and Neuroplasticity

I. Symbolic Order and Psyche

In the Buddhist or Hindu view, the self is tied to the Cosmos. Every monad, or individual soul (atman) is tied via the monadic spark to divine or collective consciousness of universal substance (Brahman), which is a higher level of the multilayered self/soul in Buddhism. This is also true for the Spinozistic monad (i.e. the monad created by the creating force God[210]) and the Leibnizian monad which reflects God, the Creator[211].

The inextricable tie between collective and individual consciousness relates to Catherine Malabou's view regarding Jacques Lacan's symbolic order. Here when we mention collective consciousness, it is Hegelian consciousness, which involves a group of beings in society at large. An individual who is

---

[210] Spinoza, *The Ethics,* p. 30: "Things were produced by God with supreme perfection"

[211] Leibniz, *Monadology,* §42: "It also follows that created things owe their perfections to the influence of God, but that they owe their imperfections to their own nature, which is incapable of being without limits. For it is in this that they are distinguished from God."

isolated becomes depressed and neurotic or perhaps even schizophrenic[212], and neuro-psychotic[213]. Mankind and its consciousness, individuated or collective, has always evolved in collectivity and hence, man becomes sick when he is an island[214]. As much as Freud differed from Jung regarding the emphasis on the scientific approach as opposed to the mythical one, Freud, like Jung, also referred to cultural symbols or archetypes, albeit at the individual level and seen in dreams[215].

---

[212] Ernest Becker, *The Denial of Death*, p. 219: We know today that the cultural sense of space, time, and perception of objects is literally built into the neural structure. As the cultural immortality ideology comes to be grounded in one's muscles and nerves, one lives it naturally, as a secure and confident part of one's daily action. We can say that the schizophrenic is deprived precisely of this neurological-cultural security against death and of programming into life. He relies instead on a hypermagnificiation of mental processes to try to secure his death transcendence; he has to try to be a hero almost entirely ideationally, from within a bad body-seating, and in a very personal way." Jon Mills, *The Unconscious Abyss*, p. 183: "The ego, beleaguered by reality, would rather retreat into its own unity, thus fleeing from the Absolute, rather than to be devoured by the collective."

[213] By neuro-psychotic, I mean mental illnesses that straddle both the neurotic and psychotic categorizations, such as borderline personality disorder and bipolar mood disorder.

[214] John Donne: "No man is an island entire of itself; every man is a piece of the continent, a part of the main"

[215] Sigmund Freud, *The Interpretation of Dreams*, p. 38.

Man's psyche is not meant to be isolated; Alfred Whitehead states, "There is no possibility of a detached, self-contained local existence," a view that applies not only to electrons but to human souls[216]. Hegel views spirit as "the universal brotherhood of man[217]." A mentally ill person is someone who denies the nature of life in the symbolic order, whether consciously and directly, or indirectly and partially; the strength of this opposition usually dictates whether they are simply neurotic or more severely ill and clinically psychotic. A depressive, for example, only ignores the symbolic order in society on a slight to moderate level. They may be irritable and anti-social. On the other hand, a paranoid schizophrenic opposes average society entirely in terms of norms, expectations, and common sense[218]. This is why many homeless people are

---

[216] Alfred Whitehead, *Modes of Thought*, p. 188
[217] H.S. Harris, *Hegel's Development: Night Thoughts*, p. 411
[218] Ernest Becker, *The Denial of Death, 63:* "The schizophrenic is supremely creative in an almost extra-human sense because he is furthest from the animal: he lacks the secure instinctive programming of lower organisms, and he lacks the secure cultural programming of average men. No wonder he appears to average men as "crazy": he is not in anything's world." Deleuze and Guattari, *Anti-Oedipus*, p. 40: "When we noted a moment ago that the schizo is at the very limit of the decoded flows of desire , we meant that he was at the very limit of the social codes, where a despotic Signifier destroys all the chains , linearizes them, biunivocalizes them, and uses the bricks as so many immobile units for the construction of an imperial Great Wall of

schizophrenic.

China. But the schizo continually detaches them , continually works them loose and carries them off in every direction in order to create a new polyvocity that is the code of desire."

II. Flexibility and Adaptation

The quantum activity or deeper level processes inside brain neurons has been discovered, and accounts for consciousness and what we call the Mind[219]. The brain is merely a quantum field, while the mind represents the quantum activity of energy in microtubules inside neurons. Brain activity is extremely complex[220]. Roger Penrose and Stuart Hameroff's theory of consciousness differs from the classical theories of neuroscience in that it holds microtubules and not neurons to be the fundamental units of the brain.

Neuroplasticity refers to the brain's ability to recover quickly and regenerate new neurons after it suffers injury. It includes to some extent neurogenesis, and the ability of the self to integrate these new neurons into its former conception of self. One question we can raise regarding Catherine Malabou's potentially infinite neuroplasticity[221] is its implications for identity;

---

[219] Elsevier, 2014

[220] Penrose, *Shadows of the Mind*, p. 9: " Moreover, on the average, there are a good deal more connections between different neurons than there are connections between transistors in a computer."

[221] Roger Penrose, *The Emperor's New Mind*, p. 397: "According to one of the long-term theories of how long-term memories are laid down, it is such changes in synaptic connections which provide the means of storing the necessary information. If this is so, then we see that brain plasticity is not an incidental complication, but an *essential* feature of the activity of the brain." Hegel, *Natural Law*, p. 484: "It is

that is, whether it can produce the creation of something that is wholly Other and new, or whether it leaves traces of an old identity, in the view of Jacques Derrida[222], who spoke of the everlasting *demeure* (the trace)[223]. Malabou, like Hegel, holds that there can be a radical Otherness in newness of a created self, so radical that Derrida would hold it up to the level of aporia.

---

necessary for individuality to advance through metamorphoses, and for all that belongs to the dominant stage to weaken and die, so that all stages of necessity appear as such stages in this individuality; but the misfortune of this period of transition (i.e. that this strengthening of the new formation has not yet cleansed itself absolutely of the past) is where the positive resides. And although nature, within a specific form, advances with a uniform (not mechanically uniform but uniformly accelerated) movement, it still enjoys a new form which it acquires. ... this emergence from the opposite out of infinity or out of its nothingness is a leap (*ein Sprung*)."

[222] To Derrida, in *the Future of Hegel*, p. 15, plasticity can also refer to "the plasticity of a form, of course, to the plasticity of another form, to the plasticity of a form involved in its process of formation, to the plasticity of the unformed, to the plasticity of 'plastic matter', but also to the plasticity of gelignite, of what can at any time explode or threaten to explode, for example, the self- identity of the present?"

[223] *Demeure*, p. 18: "Even if this meaning-to-say insists on remaining equivocal, one must nonetheless be ready to secure this equivocation to a shore, to fix or stabilize it within limits that are assured, abiding [ti demeure]."

On the individual level, the notion of self is crucially tied to memory on the subconscious level[224]; people's identities and capabilities are pliable with regard to changes in their environment, and adaptations theretoward. One thing is for sure, the brain is tied to the retention of memory associated with one's identity and homeostatic functions (waking consciousness), but not to comatose or pure consciousness. How about the memories or plasticity of someone with amnesia, or short-term memory loss?[225]

Here I will further discuss the health of the individual, whose psyche is monadic and polymorphously archetypal, the atmic center of a very large topological order of concentric circle of consciousness that culminates in Brahman and the collective Universal psyche. With regard to the symbolic order, the identity might be socially determined and constituted, as someone with Alzheimer's disease receives a jogging of memory when looking upon a

---

[224] Deleuze, *Foucault,* p. *107:* "Memory is the real name of the relation to oneself, or the affect on self by self. According to Kant, time was the form in which the mind affected itself....Time as subject, or rather subjectivation, is called memory." Yet another way in which consciousness is Deleuze's metaphysis of the fold, in the structure of memory being a self-relation.

[225] Someone with amnesia would demonstrate plasticity so radical it would be aporetic. In someone with short-term memory loss that occurs daily, there would be constant plasticity and reconstitutions of identity and self that are tied to memory, if we can call this plasticity.

familiar face of a family member. However, their ability to form new neural connections is gone. Flexibility (self-reflexivity) is a sign not only of physical health, but also of mental and neurological (brain and nervous system) health[226]. It isn't just self-awareness, but also the ability to critique oneself and be metacognitive that indicates an individual's level of health.

It is known that the brain is all we need to survive: since December 2017, there have been some successful head transplants conducted on conscious (non-comatose) but terminally ill patients. In Darwin, the fitness of an individual is its responsiveness to change, its adaptability. Formation of new neuron connections occurs with learning; the flexibility of the mind, the

---

[226] Catherine Malabou, *The Heidegger Change*, p. 272: "Man, stamping his seal everywhere, would be made master of the infinite fashionability of essences, and engage in, without completely deciding to, a series of metamorphoses in which one and the same form would be reformed, and the same pathway followed."
Lao Tzu, the Tao Te Ching, Chapter 76:
"Living plants are supple and yielding
dead branches are dry and brittle
so the hard and unyielding belong to death
and the soft and pliant belong to life
an inflexible army does not triumph
an unbending tree breaks in the wind
thus the rigid and inflexible will surely fail
while the soft and flowing will prevail."

strength of memory and self-reflexivity define mental health. The mind must be a Dionysian multiplicity as far as it is plastic and pliable[227].

Alzheimer's Disease occurs because the brain's neurons are not pliable or plastic enough. A possible treatment for the illness would be grafting stem cells and facilitating regeneration of neurons, making sure that the embodied self integrates these neurons into itself. If the brain is tied to the entire framework of the body, it isn't just the brain, but also amputated body parts that could be regenerated, or reproduced with stem cell grafting technology.

The question can be whether Catherine Malabou believes in unlimited neuroplasticity as long as we are alive. Yes, it seems for her that as long as we live, adaptation is constant with regard to change in form is optimal as a sign of health. We must believe in plasticity for those who are in their eighties in life, learning to paint or play piano. It has been found that people in their seventies generate new neurons[228] to the degree that teenagers can, and so radical plasticity is valid. We are talking about the self with integrated foreign parts (i.e. in plastic surgery). In the future, we are also integrating ourselves with AI (robot parts) and editing our DNA.

---

[227] Concerning the fold (*pli*) in Deleuze, identity is a fold because it is a self-relation. As a means of self-relating, memory is constantly being reworked and recreated by the self.
[228] *New Scientist,* April 5, 2018

Sometimes injuries rewire the brain's neurons in a good way: People struck with lightning, such as Tony Cicoria[229], became good at piano, or someone who was mugged became good at drawing geometric designs called fractals, or someone became an obsessive painter after they have a fever. These brain injuries, rather than slowing down the self, lead to rapid acceleration of plasticity while there is no negative destructive plasticity i.e. in the form of deconstitution of identity[230]. It can be a shedding of useless neurons that do not contribute to plasticity. In the case of Tony Cicoria, the energy of lightning rewired his neurons and more importantly changed the consciousness inside the neurons' microtubules.

To what extent does the self retain its essential selfhood (its identity as a citizen or past memories) but also become a more developed self, such as a tree trunk with its concentric tree rings? It would seem that there is some retention of essential selfhood. All plasticity seems to be a mediation between the Dionysian nature of breaking and scattering of the self with trauma, and an Apollonian retention of selfhood and identity[231].

---

[229] *The New Yorker,* July 23, 2007

[230] Catherine Malabou, *Forms of Living:* xix

[231] Catherine Malabou, *Ontology of the Accident,* p. 3: "Plasticity refers to an equilibrium between the receiving and giving of form. It is understood as a sort of

Plasticity is the degree to which the old self survives changes (resilience) to thrive in new environments (flexibility), as well as continue to regenerate itself (neurogenesis). A self merely does not merely build onto its preexistent neurons while retaining grasp of its former identity[232]. It is with the practice of bending that "neural muscles" become more stable. Self-reflexivity represents mental health. Perhaps the more plastic a mind is, the further it can become plastic. The more that a mind is stretched, it is more flexible.

We can look at neurosis as one form of lack of plasticity, a maladaptation. Rather than brain damage, it is merely a chemical or behavioral imbalance that can easily be righted. Neurosis is treated by therapy, where the therapist identifies the source of the trauma in the neurosis in the memory, and helps the patient reinterpret traumatic memories to overcome the trauma and live life uninhibited by a past event.

---

natural sculpting that forms our identity, an identity modeled by experience and that makes us subjects of a history, a singular, recognizable, identifiable history, with all its events, gaps, and future."

[232] Malabou, Ontology of the Accident, p. 4: "It is generally agreed that plastic construction cannot take place without a certain negativity."

III. Destructive Plasticity

It isn't just life or new creation that we have to fetishize. We have mentioned the need for destruction for creation, similar to the mention of the void and creation in Blanchot and in black holes. On the other extreme, we can have creation that is so dangerous because it is too excessive. This is the type of incomplete plasticity we see in cancer. Creation for the sole sake of growth can be likened to a cancerous tumour, or the world population multiplying while the earth has scarce resources to feed and house hungry beings. Brain cancer is negative plasticity on the side of creation.

On the one hand, we might also have plasticity where the creation of self outweighs the retention of the old identity, and this results in amnesia. There is no mediation between new and old, as the new envelops the old[233]. However, we might also have destructive plasticity in the form of brain lesions and traumas[234].

---

[233] Malabou, Ontology of the Accident, p. 9: "Destructive plasticity enables the appearance or formation of alterity where the other is absolutely lacking. Plasticity is the form of alterity when no transcendence, flight or escape is left. The only other that exists in this circumstance is being other to the self"

[234] Malabou, Ontology of the Accident, p. 3

It is only with destruction that the self can rewire itself to form its new version. Destruction or negative unity, in Hegel's words, allows the self to exercise its plasticity[235],[236].

---

[235] Hegel, *Aesthetics,* p. 144: "But subjectivity lies in the negative unity wherein differences in their real subsistence simultaneously evince themselves posited as ideal. Thus the unity of the Idea and its actuality is the negative unity of the Idea as such and its reality, as the positing and superseding of the difference between both these sides. Only in this activity is it affirmatively self-knowing, self-relating, infinite unity and subjectivity."

[236] Jon Mills, *The Unconscious Abyss,* p. 37: "The violent character of negativity, negation, and conflict is the essential driving force of the dialectic itself. In fact, for Hegel, 'being and nothing are the same' -*Science of Logic,* p. 82"

Chapter Nine. Death and Afterlife: The Beyond as Liminal

I. Bardo Theol (Tibetan Book of the Dead)

Death represents the separation of consciousness from the body[237] and the point where atman becomes Brahman, something Hegel saw as constantly equated. For Tibetans and Lamaists, the Bardo is an intermediate state between death and rebirth, a point of liberation[238]. This is somewhat similar to

---

[237] Laibl Wolf, *Practical Kabbalah*: "The most profound disintegration of the soul-body duality occurs at death. Here the dislocation of the soul from the body is so intense that only a tenuous relationship is maintained. But Kabbalah teaches that even in death a basic level of integration still exists, and the body retains its physical form. The body's progressive decay is really the loosening of this final bond ... Recordings of near death experiences have provided us with a window into the nature of the soul-body duality. In certain ways the near death phenomenon is similar to some meditative states and out-of-body experiences described in Kabbalistic literature."

[238] Donald S. Lopez, The Tibetan Book of the Dead, p. 18: "Buddhism, like several other Indian traditions, does not see death as the cessation of consciousness. Instead, death marks the dissolution of the physical elements of the person. The mental elements, generally referred to as consciousness, persist, to once again take physical form through the process of rebirth. The question arose in Indian Buddhism as to whether consciousness moves immediately to a new lifetime after death, or whether there is some intervening period."

the view of death in Maurice Blanchot as a limit-experience; a suspension of consciousness or neuter in "Literature and the Right to Death" and the inability to really die. Bardo means "between two," that is, between the states of life and physical death. There are several bardos, including one immediately following death, where one sees a lot of light, similar to what is reported in near-death experiences[239].

Donald S. Lopez, The Tibetan Book of the Dead, p. 19: " Death is not merely something to fear, but instead provides a rare opportunity in which the reality that is one's true nature, often obscured during life by the mental and physical processes that constitute the person, becomes nakedly manifest upon their dissolution. If that reality can simply be recognized, liberation is at hand."

[239] Donald S. Lopez, The Tibetan Book of the Dead, p. 19: "The first, and briefest, is the bardo of the moment of death ('chi kha' V bar do) when, at the end of a process of sensory dissolution that presages physical death, a profound state of consciousness, called the clear light, dawns. If one is able to recognize the clear light as reality, one immediately achieves liberation from saṃsāra, the cycle of rebirth. If the clear light is not recognized at that time, the consciousness of the deceased person moves into the second bardo (which appears to be a Tibetan innovation), called the bardo of reality (chos nyid bar do)."

Sam Parnia and Peter Fenwick, "Near death experiences in cardiac arrest: visions of a dying brain or visions of a new science of consciousness," p 5: "In 1975 an American doctor, Raymond Moody, published a best selling book in which he collected the experiences of 150 people who had been close to death [1]. Recurring features in their accounts included seeing a tunnel, a bright light, deceased relatives, a mystical being, entering a new domain, reaching a point of no return, a review of

II. Monads and Pure Consciousness

If consciousness is polymorphous but is in one form a type of energy, as well as bits of information trapped inside microtubules of neurons during life and released as monads into a different dimension upon death as pure consciousness. It has been previously suggested in accordance with Orchestrated objective reduction theory, that consciousness can survive beyond death somewhere in the universe in a quantum state when released from microtubules as monads. If we allow ourselves to believe that the cosmos is eternal, so is the life of the consciousness that conceives of the universe[240], like the life of the monad[241]. According to Robert Lanza, the universe is not possible without consciousness[242], and the life of the universe depends upon

---

their lives as well as 'out of body experiences' in which people described a feeling of separation from their bodies and being able to watch themselves as if from a vantage point above. These recurring features have been termed near death experiences (NDEs)."

[240] Robert Lanza, *Biocentrism*, p. 188: "The biocentric view of the timeless, spaceless cosmos of consciousness allows for no true death in any real sense. When a body dies, it does so not in the random billiard-ball matrix but in the all- is-still-inescapably-life matrix"

[241] Leibniz, Monadology, §77

[242] Robert Lanza, *Biocentrism*, p. 92: "First Principle of Biocentrism: What we perceive as reality is a process that involves our consciousness".

consciousness surviving.

Energy would simply be reorganized in a different quantum state for consciousness following death. This would explain the alternate dimensions[243] one is able to visit upon death, and many of them[244], to put it at that[245]. These

---

[243] Long and Perry, *Evidence of the Afterlife*, p. 15: "The NDERF survey asked, "Did you see or visit any beautiful or otherwise distinctive locations, levels, or dimensions? To this question 40.6 percent of NDE'ers chose "Yes." Asking this question in a more general way, the NDERF survey asked, "Did you seem to enter some other, unearthly world? To this question 52.2 percent of NDE'ers responded that they encountered an unearthly realm."

[244] Max Tegmark, *Our Mathematical Universe,* p. 401, on higher-level multiverses: "t there's a fourth level of parallel universes that's vastly larger than the three we've encountered so far, corresponding to different mathematical structures. The first three levels correspond to noncommunicating parallel universes within the same mathematical structure: Level I simply means distant regions from which light hasn't yet had time to reach us, Level II covers regions that are forever unreachable because of the cosmological inflation of intervening space, and Level III, Everett's "Many Worlds," involves noncommunicating parts of the Hilbert space of quantum mechanics. Whereas all the parallel universes at Levels I, II and III obey the same fundamental mathematical equations (describing quantum mechanics, inflation, etc.), Level IV parallel universes dance to the tunes of different equations, corresponding to different mathematical structures"

[245] Robert Lanza, *Biocentrism*, p. 92, "Can one conceive of any edges to the cosmos? Infinity? Or how particles still spring out of nothingness? Or conceive of any of the many supposed extra dimensions that must exist everywhere in order for the cosmos to consist fundamentally of interlocking strings and loops?"

realms can be compared to the bardos.

In Karma Lingpa's *Tibetan Book of the Dead*, also known as the *Profound Dharma of Self-Liberation through the Intention of the Peaceful and Wrathful Ones,* and in Tibet as *Liberation Through Hearing During the Intermediate State,* the cycle of rebirth is emphasized[246]. Since life progresses circularly back toward itself in reincarnation, death is only known as an liminal or intermediate state for the Buddhists. If we hold onto or cling to our existence, it would seem that life would be linear, and death terminal and final. However, life proceeds in a circle of rebirth[247] rather than a linear fashion proceeding from birth to death. The womb follows from the tomb; life arises from life and goes back to life, following the intermediary phase of death.

We can note the givenness of afterlife experience. Both the Tibetan book of the Dead and Near-death testimonies from the 1300 people who shared with the NDERF mention a clear light at the end of a dark tunnel, without reflection

---

[246] W.Y. Evans-Wentz, *The Tibetan Book of the Dead,* p. 39: "Buddhists and Hindus alike believe that the last thought at the moment of death determines the character of the next incarnation."

[247] T.M. Knox, *Aesthetics,* p. xi: "The true infinite is better imaged as a circle, i.e. as a line which does not go on indefinitely but returns into itself. The infinite, for Hegel, is not the boundless, but the self-bounded."

or glare[248]. Such a light is mentioned by resuscitated people who have had cardiac arrest. In Buddhist literature, light represents pure consciousness of Nirvana and a new beginning (renewal), rather than annihilation[249]. In death, pure consciousness unites everyone and everything in a state of *Brahman*.

There was one NDERF survey question that asked, "Did you pass into a tunnel or enclosure?[250]" Responses to this question are in the following graph:

---

[248] Dr. Robert Cole, NDERF.org, 1/27/2018, "At first, it was the Light, a brilliant, white light, without reflection and without glare."

[249] Long and Perry, *Evidence of the Afterlife*, p. 10: "A brilliant white light at the end of the tunnel, and when the wings enveloped me I became part of the white light. A beautiful light drew me to itself; the light still touches me with awe, and tears come immediately. At first the light was blue. Then it transitioned to white. It was an opalescent white; it almost glowed, but it did not shine. It was bright, but not intensely bright, like glowing bright--pure bright. Pure but not in the usual sense of the word. Pure as in something you've never seen before or could ever describe or put into words. It was as if we passed through a wall into my light pod directly. There was a large majestic center light and then the individual yet connected pod lights exactly like the center light only smaller. I think now the pod lights, like mine, were other souls connected to the center light, God."

[250] Long and Perry, *Evidence of the Afterlife*, p. 9: "My next awareness was of being submerged and cradled in a warm, wavy, wafting motion at the opening of a tunnel. The tunnel had billowy soft sides and was well lit, with the tunnel dimensions decreasing and brightness increasing as it got closer to a single bright light. We traveled very fast in a tunnel. The tunnel was all different colors: blue, yellow, white, green, and red."

Figure 1: Answers to "Did you pass into a tunnel or enclosure?[251]"

	Western NDE's	Non-Western NDE's
Yes	188	8
Uncertain	97	1
No	298	10

If we consider the meaning of liminality for death, it would be that dead people basically in a non-embodied coma that is only seemingly permanent, broken only by re-conception into the symbolic order on Earth via reincarnation. If energy can only change in form[252] or be reconstituted but never be annihilated or destroyed, we know that this applies also to consciousness, which is one form of energy. Reincarnation is a testament to the eternity of the soul[253]. Hence, belief in reincarnation would involve holding

---

[251] Long and Perry, *Evidence of the Afterlife,* p. 168

[252] Leibniz, *Monadology,* §72: "Thus the soul only changes body bit by bit and by degrees, so that it is never stripped of all its organs all at once. In animals there is often metamorphosis, but never metempsychosis or transmigration of souls; neither are there any entirely separate souls, nor genies without bodies."

[253] Spinoza, *Ethics,* p. 5: "Since to be finite is in fact a partial negation, and to be infinite is the absolute affirmation of the existence of some nature, it therefore follows from Prop. 7 alone that every substance must be infinite. "

faith that the soul which is reincarnated has retained its distinct identity, although it may not carry memories of its past embodiments[254]. The body might retain certain features from lifetime to lifetime, although the self might manifest into a multiplicity of ethnicities, cultures, social classes, or genders. The body also supports the notion of self as archetypal substance, displaying a number of attributes as it simply ages in one lifetime.

Levels of Heaven and Hell

The Buddhists hold to a four-tier model of the universe, comprising the four worlds of hell, the seven worlds of desires (Kama-lokas), the sixteen worlds of forms (Rupa-lokas), and the four formless worlds (Arupa-lokas). The Rupa-lokas and Kama-lokas are attainable by meditation. Kama-lokas serve as a distraction to those seeking Nirvana. The Rupa-lokas are attainable by the practice of the Four Noble Truths. The Arupa-lokas are characterized by pure

---

[254] Maurice Blanchot, *The State Not Beyond*, p. 12: "The law of the return supposing that "everything" would come again, seems to take time as completed: the circle out of circulation of all circles; but, in as much as it breaks the ring in its middle, it proposes a time not uncompleted, a time, on the contrary, finite, except in the present point that alone we think we hold, and that, lacking, introduces rupture into infinity, making us live as in a state of perpetual death."

consciousness (jhana) where perceptions cannot be grasped by the senses, but rather by the intellect[255]. They include the world of infinite space, the world of infinite consciousness, the world of emptiness or nothing, and the world of neither perception nor non-perception[256].

---

[255] It seems that the Arupa-lokas are those attained by most people in NDE's. See Chapter 10. This can explain how people perceive things without a brain.

[256] These planes would correspond to the multiverses described by Tegmark.

Chapter Ten. A Cosmophenomenology of Heaven

I. The Givenness of Near-Death Experiences

I would like to discuss the subject of pure consciousness or *jhana*: consciousness without the brain, similar to comatose consciousness. There have been thousands of near-death experiences (NDEs) reported in modern medicine, with out of body experiences (OBEs) where there is separation of consciousness from the physical body. These experiences occur with anesthesia, i.e. a medicine-induced erasure of any consciousness, and often include perception of events that happen while the person is undergoing major surgery. In accordance with Husserl's conception of the lifeworld and the subject's first-person experiences, we cannot deny the epistemological validity of these firsthand experiences. The givenness[257] of these experiences attests to

---

[257] M. Sabom, "The Near-Death Experience," p. 29: I have recently conducted a systematic investigation of these experiences in 107 persons known to have survived an episode of unconsciousness and near death (i.e. cardiac arrest and coma). Using standardized interview techniques, the social, religious, and demographic backgrounds of each person were evaluated along with the details of each medical crisis event and any possible recollections from the period of unconsciousness... I have had patients describe extensive "out of body experiences" during open heart surgery in which they observed the operation in distinct "visual" detail. ... Blacher suggests that these experiences represent a "fantasy of death" and are manifestations of a hypoxic brain attempting to deal with "the anxieties

the reality of what we may refer to as the spiritual world, an alternate world that exists when we die[258]. The experiences also attest to the fact that consciousness inscribed in monads never ceases[259],[260],[261] meaning it survives death[262]. "Researchers have concluded that NDEs may include some or all of the

---

provoked by medical procedures and talk." ... This differs from the clear "visual" perception of ongoing physical events following a loss of consciousness as found in the NDE. Moreover, many NDEs have occurred in settings far removed from "the anxieties provoked by medical procedures and talk."

[258] J.C. Eccles, *Evolution of the Brain, Creation of the Self*, p. 241: "I maintain that the human mystery is incredibly demeaned by scientific reductionism, with its claim in promissory materialism to account eventually for all of the spiritual world in terms of patterns of neuronal activity. This belief must be classed as a superstition... We have to recognize that we are spiritual beings with souls existing in a spiritual world as well as material beings with bodies and brains existing in a material world."

[259] Robert Lanza, *Biocentrism*, p. 189: "The mathematical possibility of your consciousness ending is zero"

[260] If nothingness cannot be thought, as Parmenides claimed, this could be conceptualized as the end of consciousness, which cannot occur and hence consciousness cannot be annihilated.

[261] Leibniz, *Monadology*, §70

[262] Robert Lanza, *Biocentrism*, p. 191: "If I am only my body, then I must die. If I am my consciousness, the sense of experience and sensations, then I cannot die for the simple reason that consciousness may be expressed in manifold fashion sequentially, but it is ultimately unconfined."

following twelve elements[263]: (1) Out-of-body experience (OBE): Separation of consciousness from the physical body, (2) Heightened senses, (3) Intense and generally positive emotions or feelings such as peace and bliss, (4) Passing into or through a tunnel, (5) Encountering a mystical or brilliant light, (6) Encountering other beings, either mystical beings or deceased relatives or friends, (7) A sense of alteration of time or space, (8) Life review, (9) Encountering unworldly ("heavenly") realms, (10) Encountering or learning special knowledge, (11) Encountering a boundary or barrier, and (12) A return to the body, either voluntary or involuntary".

---

[263] Long and Perry, *Evidence of the Afterlife*, p. 6

II. A Para-Phenomenology of Perception

The question arrives as to why sense experience or perception is more vivid in heaven. Is sense experience more augmented because colors and music are more diverse in heaven and that we can see hues that cannot be seen in the standard visible spectrum because we are equipped with better perceiving capacities? The answer seems to be yes to both. Colors and sounds available to us would be more diverse, as would other sensing objects, and we would have the seeing and hearing and feeling[264] ability to perceive them. "Near-death experiencers often describe their mental processes during the NDE as remarkably clear and lucid and their sensory experiences as unusually vivid, surpassing those of their normal waking state. ... Furthermore, in our collection, people reported enhanced mental functioning, significantly, more often when they were actually physiologically close to death than when they were not.[265]" This indicates that the mind (consciousness) is a separate entity

---

[264] Dr. Robert Cole, NDERF.org, January 27, 2018: "Then, the feeling... of quiet jubilation, of peace and incredible serenity enveloping me. It was not ecstasy or any feeling I could identify, except perhaps glory in the warmest most positive sense of the word. "

[265] B. Greyson, E.W. Kelly, and E.F. Kelly, "Explanatory Models for Near-Death Experiences in *The Handbook of Near-Death Experiences: Thirty Years of Investigation*, p. 229

than the body, and functions best as such.

Color perception will be five-dimensional, at least. The perceiver's range of colors, hues, shades, and perceiving range of colors seen, as well as differentiation of tones is more accurate and extensive[266]. To the ordinary person, a tetrachromat or pentachromat's account of colors is para-phenomenological or beyond describable, because the experience of color is saturated. It would be akin to a normal person describing color to a blind or colorblind person. NDE'ers, even blind or legally blind ones, have often reported normal or supernormal vision during their experience as well as in OBE's occurring in the experience where they can report what is going on in the hospital procedure. [267]

---

[266] Long and Perry, *Evidence of the Afterlife,* p. *58:* A man who experienced NDE's three times said: "The colors on the other side are the brightest colors, our most fluorescent colors on this earth are muddy [compared] to the brightness and vividness of the colors that are in Heaven." A colorblind woman who suffered a heart attack reported, "I wanted to see color again, and when I did it was fantastic! I saw colors I could never explain. A shade of red that I will never forget." Another woman who was unresponsive after a motorcycle accident said, "I was taken to a beautiful meadow with the most gorgeous plant life and colors so vibrant that I've never seen anywhere; it was amazing!"

[267] Long and Perry: "Normal and supernormal vision occurs in near-death experiences among those with significantly impaired vision or even legal blindness.

Most people with near-death experiences reported mystical beings or presences, often described as angels and resembling loved ones who had passed on, but not necessarily having wings[268]. Communication between beings is done by telepathy[269]. Perhaps telepathy is all the more facilitated by the fact that consciousness as quantum activity is not confined to the space of brain neurons, and so quantum entanglement is constantly occurring in free space. This would also imply perpetual or constant synchronicity and entanglement of quantum information in these Brahmanically structured "minds".

Several NDE'ers who were blind from birth have reported highly visual near-death experiences."

[268] Long and Perry, p. 130: "To the question, "Did you seem to encounter a mystical being or presence?" NDE'ers responded with 49.9% selecting "Definite being, or voice clearly of mystical or otherworldly origin," while 9.8 percent selected "Unidentifiable voice," and 40.3 percent selected "Neither."

[269] Long and Perry, p. 132: "On the other side communication is done via telepathy (thought transfer)", said a man referred to as Leonard who had had a heart attack. Long and Perry, p. 62: "All sound was incredibly clear. The voice of the Supreme Being seemed to emanate from nowhere but at the same time from everywhere. Words did not come from the mouths of beings, but from the aura around them."

60.5 percent of those interviewed answered yes to the question, "Did you have any sense of altered space or time.[270]" 33.9 percent of those interviewed answered yes to "Did time seem to speed up?" and selecting "Everything seemed to be happening all at once[271]." The fact that of those interviewed, everyone described their experiences slightly differently suggests that people visited different realms or dimensions of heaven; that as in Western religious cosmology, heaven is multi-dimensional[272]. If consciousness necessitates a dimension or realm, there are virtually an infinite number of parallel worlds

---

[270] Long and Perry, *Evidence of the Afterlife,* p. 13: "Both time and space in earth stopped completely. Simultaneously, "the time and the space" on the other side was completely alive, evidential, and real. Yet, while I was in the light, I had ... no sense of time as I know it here on Earth. In other words, no sense of the serial nature of time... past, present, or future. All times (past, present, and future) were experienced at every moment in time while I was in the light."

[271] Ralph Waldo Emerson, "The Over-Soul," "The soul circumscribes all things. As I have said, it contradicts all experience. In like manner it abolishes time and space." Lord Byron, Cain, "Spirits / Can crowd eternity into an hour, / Or stretch an hour to eternity"

[272] Leibniz, *Monadology, §57*: "In the same way it happens that, because of the infinite multitude of simple substances, there are just as many different universes, which are nevertheless merely perspectives of a single universe according to the different points of view of each monad."

where this could occur, qua the infinitely occurring expansion of space mentioned in Chapter I.

III. Refuting the Skeptics

The skeptics' suggestion that NDE'ers expect to see these deceased beings cannot explain NDEs in which the NDEr had never met the deceased or did not even know the person was deceased at the time of the NDE. Although near-death experiences can be reproduced on a chemical level by ketamine[273]This does not detract from the fact that all near-death experiences reported were naturally occurring without the presence of ketamine, and often in states like neuroscientist Eben Alexander's, where the subject was braindead and without a functioning brain (cortex). Any chemical effects would imply a functioning brain. Hence it would disprove statements such as "Within a scientific paradigm, it is not possible that the "spirit rises out of the body, leaving the brain behind, but somehow still incorporating neuronal functions such as sight, hearing, and proprioception[274]". This is not true. Because we do

---

[273] Karl L. Jansen, *The Journal of Near-Death Studies,* p. 5: "Near-death experiences (NDEs) can be reproduced by ketamine via blockade of receptors in the brain for the neurotransmitter glutamate, the N-methyl-D-aspartate (NMDA) receptors. Conditions that precipitate NDEs, such as hypoxia, ischemia, hypoglycemia, and temporal lobe epilepsy, have been shown to release a flood of glutamate, overactivating NMDA receptors and resulting in neurotoxicity. Ketamine prevents this neurotoxicity."

[274] Morse, 1989, p. 225, Henri Bergson, *Matter and Memory, p.* 235, my emphasis: "But, as long as we confine ourselves to sensation and to pure perception, we can

have an organic process of the chemical dimethyltryptamine occurring naturally in the brain during and throughout our lives, as well as at death, we can still say that death or the process of dying is biochemical. Based upon givenness as an epistemological method, near-death experiences are true experiences of the lifeworld and death[275] that demonstrate consciousness as an

---

hardly be said to be dealing with the spirit. No doubt we demonstrate, in opposition to the theory of an epiphenomenal consciousness, that *no cerebral state is the equivalent of a perception*....to touch the reality of spirit we must place ourselves at the point where an individual consciousness, continuing and retaining the past in a present enriched by it, thus escapes the law of necessity... when we pass from pure perception to memory, we definitely abandon matter for spirit." To trust in the faculty of memory, i.e. in the testimony of those such as Eben Alexander who had an NDE, is to abide by the epistemological method of Husserlian givenness for the lifeworld. Deleuze and Guattari, *What is Philosophy,* p. 210: "Thought, even in the form it actively assumes in science, does not depend upon a brain made up of organic connections and integrations: according to phenomenology, thought depends on man's relations with the world-with which the brain is necessarily in agreement because it is drawn from these relations, as excitations are drawn from the world and reactions from man, including their uncertainties and failures. "Man thinks, not the brain"; but this ascent of phenomenology beyond the brain toward a Being in the world, through a double criticism of mechanism and dynamism, hardly gets us out of the sphere of opinions."

[275] Robyn Horner, *In Excess,* p. xv: "Further, while what gives itself will often necessarily first show itself, events like death or birth actually only show themselves

ontological constant[276], one that never goes out of being but which can only be restructured[277] in a different dimension without losing its essential properties. Especially in the case of the brain-dead, blind, or anesthetized and unconscious, it shows that consciousness has separated from the body but still has a biophysical basis. In the view of Penrose and Hameroff, consciousness is released from the microtubules of the brain and into the universe, in a state of Brahman, as a group of monads that by their essence as monads inscribe information fundamental to retaining the soul's structure.

---

in the mode of being given. The event is a *fait accompli*, irremediably striking the one who receives it."

[276] Leibniz, *Monadology*, §77: "It may be said not only that the soul (mirror of an indestructible universe) is indestructible"

[277] Leibniz, *Monadology*, §72: "The soul only changes body bit by bit and by degrees"

Chapter Eleven. Conclusions

This chapter traces the main arguments listed throughout chapter one to ten, and also includes their conclusions.

Chapter I.

1. I speak about the limits of materialism in discussing the 96% of the universe that is not ordinary (baryonic) matter. This includes the dark energy (68-70% of the universe) that is said to expand galaxies apart and is present as consciousness in quantum physics.

2. Both Heisenberg's Uncertainty Principle as well as Einstein's Relativity emphasizes the fault of anthropocentrism, which wrongly places humans in the position of absolute certainty or infallibility regarding measurement.

3. In a position called panenpsychism, the energy of consciousness is potentially in all things, and all things could be conscious but this is not totally the case. Panenpsychism is a type of vitalism. When we talk about the ubiquity of energy in this world, we should focus on its behavior, whether it is harmonic or anharmonic, before we determine whether the energy is alive.

Chapter II.

1. When we talk about consciousness as a constant in the universe, the phenomenological approach that emphasizes the primacy of the Lebenswelt or Lifeworld in Husserl is used. The lifeworld includes the horizon of the "I" but does not limit itself to perception within the horizon of the "I". With cosmophenomenology, we talk about collective consciousness and quantum consciousness, that is, consciousness from the standpoint of quantum physics.

2. Dark energy, by being responsible for the relativity of spacetime, has been said to be a cosmological constant that can survive in a void or black hole. Energy has been said to be a fundamental constant in the universe, according to the equation $E=MC^2$. This describes the relation between ordinary energy/matter as well as dark energy/matter. Energy is neither destroyed nor created, but simply changes form into other types of energy or into matter. Matter is secondary to energy. The ontological constancy (fundamental) of consciousness would mean that consciousness would also survive death in some form.

3. The survival of consciousness beyond death cannot be explained

by classical physics which is applicable to ordinary matter, but rather only by quantum physics which regards the energy fields underlying atoms. In the theory of Hameroff and Penrose, where consciousness occurs as the quantum activity in microtubules within neurons, the basic framework for the soul or consciousness constituting quantum information would survive upon death

4. Consciousness can be quantum entangled and is not limited by the laws of spacetime or matter (locality). This displays the fact that consciousness is not matter, but rather, a type of energy.

5. Consciousness, expressible in biophotons as a form of light, is energy.

6. Consciousness, as a form of polymorphous yet-to-be-categorized life-related dark energy is a constant in the universe; neither coming or going into being but merely changing form.

7. Will or consciousness is a physically detectible energy that interacts with the world. Although this does not agree with the traditional meaning of materialism, it is a type of physicalism.

Chapter III.

1. Consciousness is the anharmonic activity that occurs in microtubules inside brain neurons, and is released from these neurons at death, passing from an atmic to Brahmanic state as quantum information-inscribing dark energy that does not need to be housed by neurons. This is how it survives death. Like Leibniz's monad, the content of the microtubules is indestructible. Basically, consciousness can exist in a Brahmanic pure form as wave energy that is dark; without the body, functioning brain, or activity of brain cells normally responsible for waking consciousness.
2. According to Leibniz there is pre-established harmony between all substances in the universe. This applies to the way that the soul influences the body in a type of interactionism that is intra-substantial rather than inter-causal.
3. Leibniz's harmony can be contrasted from Goethe's total harmony of the spheres both in scope as well as in totality. Leibniz's harmony of affirmation includes room for anharmonic inside microtubules as well as disharmony in the process of reaching an overall harmony.
4. The soul or psyche can be considered archetypal in form and structure, in terms of the way that it can then change according to a set pattern.

This includes the way that energies of consciousnesses are quantum-entangled.

Chapter IV.

1. I further discuss the application of the First Thermodynamic law concerning energy to the scientific phenomenon of consciousness, which states that consciousness as energy can neither be created nor destroyed. It must only change form between higher and lower order states at all stages of its physical composition. That means that all we are essentially looking at in the universe are changes of energy (not matter, as the materialist claims). We can take into the concentration of energy and the frequency of such energy, along with the types of matter or condensed energy in its composition. (The essence of a thing metaphysically is dependent specifically on the configuration of space-time and frequency of quantum vibrations as well as condensation of energy into substances).

2. At the micro level of the universe it seems that it is only at times that there is activity at the micro level of the universe that proceeds as if orchestrated. For consciousness, described as anharmonic vibrations, there is still total orchestration via synaptic outputs.

3. At the macro level of the universe we must look at conditions of singularity and display disharmony and lack of physical regularity of

matter, time and space. Goethe's harmony of spheres only applies to certain points of space in the universe that do not appear as a black hole from outside.

4. At the micro level it is partially disharmonic, as it is at the macro level.
5. It would be improper to characterize a photon or wave as a multiplicity because its sporadic changes would be characterized too broadly. However, we can say that consciousness is a multiplicity insofar as it is dark energy changing frequencies and constantly being entangled.
6. The wave-particle duality or complementarity can be conceived of as a paradox.

Chapter V.

1. There exist an infinite number of universes, or multiverses, in which the ideal happens. According to Leibniz, what is happening in this particular world is said to be the best possible situation that can happen given the constraints of space and time applying to the world. If space is not a constant, it is in dimensions not confined by the typical definition of space that the soul as quantum information can inhabit and visit, while a space shuttle cannot. The view of multiple worlds or universes plays a role in the theory of Quantum Immortality and the Many Minds Approach, which have been discussed by the physicists Max Tegmark, Michael Lockwood, and Hans Moravec, among others.
2. The question remains if there is multiplicity in Brahman.
3. The majority of the Milky Way Galaxy is not baryonic matter, but rather, dark matter.
4. We may approach the phenomenon of consciousness as dark energy's process of inscription and manifestation of information in space-time, sometimes interacting with ordinary matter. As we bridge physics with metaphysics we may surmise that consciousness does not only arise from the information dynamics

of spacetime, but as dark energy is actually fundamental to the ordering and dynamics of reality itself in some ways. Space is said to be fractal and time is also fractally recursive. The life of a biological being represents a path of recursive feedback operations throughout the spatiotemporal dimension, progressing from a unique encoded set of directions in the form of space-time coordinates onto a holographic spacememory field that is morphogenetic and maintains coherency in the vastly unified spatiotemporal network.

Chapter VI.

1. The universe emerged in a set of conditions where there was no time or space, matter or energy,, or gravity. Matter remained infinitely condensed, as in a black hole. We can liken void space to creation. Void spaces such as black holes demonstrate that the universe is ordered in harmony except for sites where there are perturbations in the harmonic function and matter is being reconfigured. In void spaces, we would have both undoing and annihilation of the material before creation would begin anew.

2. The quantum information that consciousness disperses into upon death has been compared to Blanchot's neuter, and demonstrates the impossibility of death. The defining essence of Blanchot's neuter is in the way that it critiques the notion of presence and ultimately displaces the subject who writes, which also displaces the idea of the subject as a locus of self-presence. We can compare the neuter to multiplicity or Brahman as the neuter might place itself in dialectical opposition to the One, thus including itself conveniently in the whole. For Blanchot, writing establishes a relation with alterity that would appear to be strictly impersonal; one of exteriority. We can also regard the will to

annihilation or non-ego in the neuter as important for self-development or self-actualization, much as a seeming annihilation must occur for there to be an alterity or reconstitution of elements or matter in a black hole. Dark energy is notable because due to its effect of repelling gravity, it is the only substance in the universe that can survive a black hole.

Chapter. VII.

We can see parallels in collective spirit in the thought of Hegel, Emerson, and Benjamin.

1. Georg W.F. Hegel's thought shows similarities to Vedanta Hinduism, especially regarding Spirit and self. However, Hegel was wary of how Indian cult religion was a detriment toward human freedom. Hegel equates atman and Brahman.
2. Ralph Waldo Emerson portrays the over-soul as the collective soul or Brahman, referring to it as "that Unity, that Over-soul, within which every man's particular being is contained and made one with all other" ("The Over-Soul")
3. Walter Benjamin also described the soul as collective, in terms of its changes as a whole, and the self-consciousness of collective humanity increases or becomes more saturated throughout history in Erfahrung and Jetztzeit (the spontaneous now-moment of experiencing) as opposed to Erleben (passive and inauthentic experience).

Chapter 8.

1. In the Buddhist or Hindu view, the self is tied to the Cosmos or Collective Self. This is also true for the Spinozistic monad (i.e. the monad created by the creating force God) and the Leibnizian monad which reflects God, the Creator. Likewise, there is an inextricable tie or relation between collective and individual consciousness in Jacques Lacan's symbolic order. Like the Hegelian Spirit, the symbolic order involves a group of beings in society at large.

2. One question we can raise regarding Catherine Malabou's potentially infinite neuroplasticity, is its implications for identity; that is, whether it can produce the creation of something that is wholly Other and new, or whether it leaves traces of an old identity, in the view of Jacques Derrida, who spoke of the everlasting demeure (the trace). Malabou, like Hegel, holds that there can be a radical Otherness in newness of a created self, so radical that Derrida would hold it up to the level of aporia. We can contrast health as neuroplasticity from diseases like Alzheimer's.

3. Hegel in the *Aesthetics* discusses the importance of negative unity

in a subject's development. Destruction allows the self to exercise its plasticity. Hence, plasticity is a dialectic between growth and destruction, as what is extrinsic to the self's health is pruned away.

Chapter IX.

1. For Tibetans and Lamaists, the Bardo is an intermediate state between death and rebirth, a point of liberation. This is somewhat similar to the view of death in Maurice Blanchot as a limit-experience; a suspension of consciousness or neuter and the inability to really die.

2. It has been previously suggested in accordance with Orchestrated objective reduction theory, that consciousness can survive beyond death somewhere in the universe in a quantum state when released from microtubules as monads. If we allow ourselves to believe that the cosmos is eternal, so is the life of the consciousness that conceives of the universe, like the life of the monad. According to Robert Lanza, the universe is not possible without consciousness, and the life of the universe depends upon consciousness surviving. Energy would simply be reorganized in a different quantum state for consciousness following death. This would explain the alternate dimensions one is able to visit upon death.

Overall Main Conclusions

A. Consciousness displays multiple properties of energy.

B. As energy, consciousness is eternal and imperishable.

C. The universe is harmonic and anharmonic at the quantum level as well as at the macro-cosmological level.

D. Consciousness as dark energy is a cosmological constant.

E. The information dynamics involved in the processes of consciousness and the dynamics involved in engendering the defining characteristics of space, time, energy and matter are one and the same in a symphony that is both harmonic and anharmonic.

F. As we bridge physics with metaphysics we may surmise that consciousness does not only arise from the information dynamics of spacetime, but as dark energy is actually fundamental to the ordering and dynamics of reality itself.

Bibliography

Alexander, Eben. *Proof of Heaven: A Neurosurgeon's Journey into the Afterlife.* New York:Simon and Schuster. 2012.

Aristotle. *On the Soul, Book I.* Translated by J.A. Smith. Cambridge: Cambridge University Press. 1994.

Aristotle. *On the Soul (Books I, II, and III).* Translated by W.S. Hett. Cambridge: Harvard University Press. 1936.

Arstila, Valtteri, and Lloyd, Dan. *Subjective Time: The Philosophy, Psychology, and Neuroscience of Temporality.* Cambridge: MIT Press. 2014.

Ashton, Anthony. *Harmonograph: A Visual Guide to the Mathematics of Music.* Glastonbury: Wooden Books, Limited. 2005.

Becker, Ernest. *The Denial of Death.* New York: Free Press. 1997.

Bergson, Henri. *Duration and Simultaneity.* Translated by Leon Jacobson. Indianapolis: The Bobbs-Merrill Company, Inc. 1965.

Bergson, Henri. *Matter and Memory.* Translated by N. Margaret Paul and W. Scott Palmer. New York: Dover Publications. 2004.

Blanchot, Maurice. *Thomas the Obscure.* Translated by Robert Lamberton. New

York: Station Hill Press. 1973.

Blanchot, Maurice. *The Step Not Beyond.* Translated by Lycette Nelson. Albany: State University of New York. 1992.

Blanqui, Louis-Auguste. *Eternity by the Stars.* Translated by Frank Chouraqui. New York: Contra Mum Press. 2013.

Bohm, David. *Wholeness and the Implicate Order.* London: Routledge. 1980.

Bousso, Raphael. "The Cosmological Constant Problem, Dark Energy, and the Landscape of String Theory." Lawrence Berkeley National Library. 2007.

Burnet, John. *Early Greek Philosophy,* Third ed. Whitefish, Montana: Kessinger Publishing. 2003.

Chalmers, David. "The Hard Problem of Consciousness" in the Blackwell Companion to Consciousness, Edited by Max Velmans and Susan Schneider, p. 225, Wiley-Blackwell. 2007.

Chown, Marcus. "Dying to Know: Would you lay your life on the line for a theory? Marcus Chown meets a man who is thinking about it." *New Scientist,* December 20, 1997.

Deleuze and Guattari. *Anti-Oedipus: Capitalism and Schizophrenia.* Translated by Robert Hurley. New York: Penguin. 2009.

Deleuze and Guattari. *What is Philosophy?* Translated by Hugh Tomlinson and Graham Burchell. New York: Columbia University Press. 1991.

Deleuze, Gilles. *Foucault.* Translated by Sean Hand. Minneapolis: University of Minnesota Press, 1st ed. 1988.

Derrida, Jacques. *Demeure: Fiction and Testimony.* Translated by Elizabeth Rottenberg. Stanford: Stanford University Press. 1998.

Descartes, Rene. *Meditations* in *The Philosophical Works of Descartes.* Trans. Elizabeth Haldane. Cambridge: Cambridge University Press. 1911.

Eccles, J.C. *Evolution of the Brain, Creation of the Self.* London: Routledge, 1991.

Emerson, Daniel et al. "Direct modulation of microtubule stability contributes to anthracene general anesthesia." J Am Chem Soc 2013;135(14):5398. 2013.

Epperson, Michael. *Quantum Mechanics and the Philosophy of Alfred North Whitehead.* New York: Fordham University Press. 2004.

Fisher, David et al. A human brain network derived from coma-causing brainstem lesions. American Academy of Neurology. 2016.

Freud, Sigmund. The Interpretation of Dreams. Translated by James Strachey. Philadelphia: Basic Books. 2010.

Ghosh Subrata et al. "Design and Construction of a Brain-Like Computer: A New Class of Frequency: Fractal Computing Using Wireless Communication in a Supramolecular Organic, Inorganic System." Information 5(1):28-100 doi:10.3390/info5010028. 2014.

Goethe, Johann Wolfgang von. *Faust.* Translated by George Madison Priest. Chicago: Encyclopedia Britannica, Inc. 1977.

Goethe, Johann Wolfgang von. *Faust.* Translated by Bayard Taylor. New York: Houghton Mifflin. 1870.

Greyson, Bruce et al. "Explanatory Models for Near-Death Experiences," in *The Handbook of Near-Death Experiences: Thirty Years of Investigation,* ed. J. Holden, B. Greyson, and D. James. Westerport, Connecticut: Praeger Publishers, 2009.

Hameroff, Stuart and Chopra, Deepak. "The Quantum Soul: A Scientific Hypothesis. Chapter 5 in *Mindfulness in Behavioral Health.* New York: Springer.

Hameroff, Stuart and Penrose, Roger. "Consciousness in the universe: A review of the 'Orch OR' theory." dx.doi.org/10.1016/j.plrev.2013.08.002. 2014.

Hameroff, Stuart and Penrose, Roger. "Reply to criticism of the 'Orch OR qubit'–'Orchestrated objective reduction' is scientifically justified." dx.doi.org/10.1016/j.plrev.2013.11.00

Hameroff, Stuart and Penrose, Roger. "Reply to seven commentaries on "Consciousness in the universe: Review of the 'Orch OR' theory." dx.doi.org/10.1016/j.plrev.2013.08.002. 2013.

Hegel, Georg W.F. *Aesthetics: Lectures on Fine Art.* Translated by T.M. Knox. Oxford: Clarendon Press. 1975.

Hegel, Georg W.F. *Hegel's Philosophy of Nature,* Part Two of *Encyclopedia of the Philosophical Sciences.* Oxford: Clarendon Press. 2004.

Hegel, Georg W.F. *Natural Law.* Translated by T. M. Knox, introduction by H. B. Acton. Philadelphia: University of Pennsylvania Press. 1975.

Hegel, Georg W.F. *The Phenomenology of Mind.* Translated by Baillie, James Black. London: S. Sonnenschein. 1910.

Hegel, Georg W.F. *On the Orbits of the Planets.* Translated by David Healan. Berlin: 2006.

Heisenberg, Werner. *Physics and Philosophy: The Revolution in Modern Science.* London: Penguin Books. 2000.

Hollingdale, R.J. *Nietzsche, The Man and His Philosophy*, Cambridge: Cambridge University Press. 2001.

Houlgate, Stephen, ed. *Hegel and the Philosophy of Nature.* Albany: State University of New York Press. 1998.

Husserl, Edmund. *Crisis of European Sciences and Transcendental Phenomenology.* Translated by David Carr. Evanston: Northwestern Press. 1970.

Husserl, Edmund. *Logische Untersuchungen. Zweiter Teil: Untersuchungen zur Phänomenologie und Theorie der Erkenntnis.* Halle a.S.: Max Niemeyer, 1901.

Huygens, Christiaan. *Treatise on Light.* Translated by Sylvanus P. Thompson. Chicago: University of Chicago Press. 2005.

Issaeva, Elmira A., "Human Perception of Physical Experiments and the Simplex Interpretation of Quantum Physics." Progress in Physics Vol. 1, 47-51.

Janse, Karl L. R. "The Ketamine Model of the Near-Death Experience: A Central Role for the N-Methyl-D-Aspartate Receptor." Journal of Near-Death Studies, 16(10) Fall 1997.

Jung, Carl Gustav & Pauli, Wolfgang. *Atom and Archetype: The Pauli/Jung*

Letters, 1932-1958. Translated by David Roscoe. Princeton: Princeton University Press. 2014.

Jung, Carl G. *Synchronicity: An Acausal Connecting Principle.* Translated by R.F.C. Hull. Bollingen, Switzerland: Bollingen Foundation. 1993.

Keen, Jeffrey S. "Communicating with Plants." *The Journal of the World Institute for Scientific Exploration,* Vol. 3 No. 3. 3 July 2014.

Kennedy, Barbara. "Discovered: Why warm galaxies stop birth of new stars." *Penn State News.* May 25, 2016. http://news.psu.edu/story/412399/2016/05/25/research/discovered-why-warm-galaxies-stop-birth-new-stars

Kim, Jaegwon. "Making Sense of Emergence" in *Emergence: Contemporary Readings in Philosophy and Science,* Edited by Mark A. Bedau and Paul Humphreys. MIT Press. 2008.

Kouwn, Seyen, et al. "Massive photon and dark energy." Phys. Rev. D Vol. 93, 2016.

Kozhevnikov, Maria, Elliot, James, Shephard, Jennifer, and Gramann, Klaus. "Neurocognitive Temperature and Somatic Components of Temperature Increases during g-Tummo Meditation: Legend and Reality." March 29, 2013. https://doi.org/10.1371/journal.pone.0058244

Laager, Frederik. *Sources and functions of ultra-weak photon emission.* Seoul National University, Seoul, Korea. 2008.

Lao Tzu. *Tao Te Ching.* Trans. James Legge. La Vergne, Tennessee: BN Publishing. 2007.

Lanza, Robert. *Biocentrism: How Life and Consciousness are the Keys to Understanding the True Nature of the Universe.* Dallas: Ben Bella Books: 2010.

Leibniz, Gottfried Wilhelm. *The Monadology and Other Philosophical Writings.* Translated by Robert Latta. Oxford: Clarendon Press. 1898.

Leibniz, Gottfried Wilhelm. *Theodicy.* Translated by E.M. Hubbard. Oxford: Bibliobazaar. 2005.

Lingpa, Karma. *The Tibetan Book of the Dead: The Great Book of Natural Liberation Through Understanding in the Between.* Translated by Robert Thurman. New York: Bantam Books. 1993.

Lockwood, Michael. *Mind, Brain, and the Quantum: The Compound 'I'.* Hoboken: Wiley-Blackwell, 1989.

Long, Jeffrey and Perry, Paul. *Evidence of the Afterlife: The Science of Near-Death Experiences.* New York: Harper One. 2011.

Malabou, Catherine. Translated by Lisbeth During. *The Future of Hegel:*

Plasticity, Temporality, and Dialectic. London: Routledge. 2005.

Malabou, Catherine. Translated by Peter Skafish. *The Heidegger Change: On the Fantastic in Philosophy.* Albany: State University of New York Press. 2004.

Malabou, Catherine. Translated by Steven Miller. *The New Wounded: From Neurosis to Brain Damage (Forms of Living).* New York: Fordham University Press. 2012.

Malabou, Catherine. Trans. Carolyn Shread. *Ontology of the Accident: An Essay on Destructive Plasticity.* Malden: Polity Press. 2012.

Marion, Jean-Luc.*In Excess: Studies of Saturated Phenomena*, Fordham University Press, 2002.

Mcrae, Mike. "Quantum Weirdness Once Again Shows We're Not Living in a Computer Simulation." 29 Sept 2017. http://www.sciencealert.com/quantum-complexity-rules-out-our-universe-as-a-computer-simulation?utm_content=buffer020af&utm_medium=social&utm_source=twitter.com&utm_campaign=buffer

Mills, Jon. *The Unconscious Abyss: Hegel's Anticipation of Psychoanalysis.* Albany: SUNY Press. 2002.

Morse, M. L. Comments on "A neurobiological model for near-death experiences." Journal of Near-Death Studies, 7, 1989, 223-228.

Mureika, Jonas and Stojkovic, Dejan. "Detecting Vanishing Dimensions via Primordial Gravitational Wave Astronomy. Physical Review Letters." 2011; 106 (10) DOI: 10.1103/PhysRevLett.106.101101

Nietzsche, Friedrich. *The Gay Science.* Translated by Walter Kaufmann. New York: Random House. 1974.

Nietzsche, Friedrich. *The Will to Power.* Translated by Walter Kaufmann and R.J. Hollingdale. New York: Random House. 1967.

Overbye, Dennis. "Have Dark Forces Been Messing With the Cosmos?" *The New York Times.* February 25, 2019.

Pascal, Blaise. *The Thoughts of Blaise Pascal.* Translated from the text of W. Auguste Molinier. London: Bell and Sons. 1901.

Penrose, Roger. *The Emperor's New Mind.* New York: Penguin Books. 1991.

Penrose, Roger. *The Nature of Space and Time.* Princeton: Princeton University Press. 2010.

Penrose, Roger and Hameroff, Stuart. "Discovery of Quantum Vibrations in

"Microtubules Inside Brain Neurons Corroborates Controversial 20-Year-Old Theory of Consciousness." https://www.elsevier.com/about/press-releases/research-and-journals/discovery-of-quantum-vibrations-in-microtubules-inside-brain-neurons-corroborates-controversial-20-year-old-theory-of-consciousness. January 16, 2014. Date Accessed January 14, 2018.

Penrose, Roger. *The Road to Reality: A Complete Guide to the Laws of the Universe.* New York: Vintage Books. 2007.

Penrose, Roger. *Shadows of the Mind: A Search for the Missing Science of Consciousness.* Oxford: Oxford University Press. 1994.

Perkins, Franklin. *Leibniz and China: A Commerce of Light.* Cambridge University Press, 2004.

Plato. *Five Dialogues.* Translated by G.M.A. Grube. Indianapolis: Hackett. 1981.

Plato, *The Symposium*, Greek text with commentary by Kenneth Dover. Cambridge: Cambridge University Press, 1980.

Plotnitsky, Arkady. *Chaosmologies: Quantum Field Theory, Chaos and Thought in Deleuze and Guattari's What is Philosophy?* Paragraph 29:2 (2006) 40–56.

Plotnitsky, Arkady. *Complementarity: Anti-Epistemology after Bohr and Derrida.* Durham: Duke University Press, 1994.

Plotnitsky, Arkady. *Epistemology and Probability: Bohr, Heisenberg, Schrodinger, and the Nature of Quantum-Theoretical Thinking.* New York: Springer. 2010.

Popp, Fritz-Albert, "Properties of Biophotons and their Theoretical Implications," Indian Journal of Experimental Biology, Vol. 41, May 2003, p. 391-402.

Popp, Fritz-Albert, Nagi W, Li KH, Scholz W, Weingartner O, Wolf R. Biophoton emission. New evidence for coherence and DNA as source. Cell Biophys. 1984;6: 33–51.

Quine, W.V.O.. "Two Dogmas of Empiricism." The Philosophical Review 60, 1951: 20-43.

Radin, Dean et al. "Consciousness and the double-slit interference pattern: Six experiments." *Physics Essays* 25, 2 (2012).

Robson, David. "Brain 'entanglement could explain memories." *New Scientist,* January 2010. https://www.newscientist.com/article/dn18371-brain-entanglement-could-explain-memories.

Sabom, Michael. "The Near-Death Experience," *Journal of the American Medical Association* 244, no. 1 (1980).

Sagan, Carl. *Billions and Billions: Thoughts on Life and Death at the Brink of the Millennium.* New York: Ballantine Books. 1997.

Sagan, Carl. *Cosmos.* New York: Random House. 1980.

Sellars, *Empiricism and the Philosophy of Mind.* Cambridge: Harvard Univ. Press. 1997.

Schaya, Leo. *The Universal Meaning of the Kabbalah.* Sydney: Allen and Unwin. 1971.

Schopenhauer, Arthur. *The World as Will and Representation,* Volume 1. Translated by E.F.J. Payne. New York: Dover Publications. 1969.

Schopenhauer, Arthur. *The World as Will and Representation.* Volume II. Translated by E.F.J. Payne. New York: Dover Publications. 1966.

Spinoza. *The Ethics.* Edited and Translated by G.H.R. Parkinson. Oxford: Oxford University Press. 2000.

Strassburg, Marc. "Body temperature changes during the practice of g Tum-mo yoga." *Nature* Vol.298, p. 402 (22 July 1982). doi:10.1038/298402b0

Teubner, Jonathan. *A Macat Analysis of St. Augustine's Confessions.* New York: Routledge. 2017.

Tegmark, Max. "Consciousness as a State of Matter." *Chaos, Solitons & Fractals*, March 17, 2015.

Tegmark, Max. "The Interpretation of Quantum Mechanics: Many Worlds or Many Words?" in *Fundamental Problems in Quantum Theory*, eds. M.H. Rubin and Y.H. Shih. Hoboken: Wiley 1997.

Tegmark, Max. *Our Mathematical Universe: My Quest for the Ultimate Nature of Reality*. New York: Alfred A. Knopf. 2014.

Through the Wormhole. Hosted by Morgan Freeman. Science Channel, June 8, 2011.

Velmans, Max and Schneider, Susan, ed. *The Blackwell Companion to Consciousness,* 1st ed. Hoboken: Blackwell Publishing. 2007.

Whitehead, Alfred North. *Modes of Thought,* New York: Macmillan. 1938.

Whitehead, Alfred North. *Process and Reality*, New York City: Macmillan Limited. 1929.

www.ingramcontent.com/pod-product-compliance
Lightning Source LLC
Chambersburg PA
CBHW071707090426
42738CB00009B/1692